From EDEN to ETERNITY

To Judy
— Tom Williams

Rarely have I encountered a man so genuine and godly as Tom Williams. One meeting with him and you're impressed with his love for people and his love for the Word. Those two passions have combined to lead him to write this book. I've had the privilege of witnessing what Tom can do to the cover of a book with his art — now we'll enjoy what Tom has done to the message of this book with his wisdom.   —*Max Lucado*

T. M. WILLIAMS

From EDEN to ETERNITY

THE
CHRISTIAN JOURNEY
THROUGH TIME

COLLEGE PRESS PUBLISHING COMPANY • JOPLIN, MISSOURI

Library of Congress Cataloging-in-Publication Data

Williams, T.M. (Thomas Myron), 1941–
    From Eden to eternity: the Christian journey through time /
T.M. Williams.
      p.   cm.
    ISBN 0-89900-789-9 (pbk.)
    1. Theology, Doctrinal—Popular works. I. Title
BT77.W58 1997
230—dc21   97-19152
                                                         CIP

This book is affectionately
dedicated to my parents
Tommy and Lucy Williams
whose life and influence
gave me a hunger for
things eternal.

Table of Contents

Foreword

This is a simple book with a simple purpose — to give the reader an understandable, easy-to-follow overview of the content and meaning of Christianity. I looked for such a book as this to use in my own teaching of the facts and meaning of The Faith in a systematic and interesting way. Of course, books on systematic theology were available, but they seemed to be written for systematic theologians. I felt that there should be a book that could be easily understood by the layman in the pew, the new Christian without a background in The Faith, the would-be Christian checking out the rationality of our beliefs, or the long-time Christian who has somehow failed to connect all the dots of doctrine into a clear picture. So, rushing in where angels fear to tread, I decided to tackle the task myself. I pounded into my Macintosh everything I knew about Christian theology, and out came this book.

This book is as simply written and direct as I know how to make it. I may as well admit that it is a book on systematic theology. Its purpose is to help the reader understand the great Christian doctrines of Redemption, Justification, Reconciliation, Sanctification, and Atonement. But unless my fingers have slipped on the keyboard, this is the only time you will see these words in these pages.

I could never understand why some Christians seem to think theology is dull. It is dramatic and fascinating and a cause for cosmic wonder. And it hones in on the very essence of reality. My aim in this book is to convey the drama of God's dealings with man while helping readers know what they believe and why. I want to present theology not as a system of dry, academic concepts, but as a story. The story begins with creation and moves chronologically to the end times. But the narrative does not always stay right on the main road; it takes scenic bypasses now and then. When we come to a subject that inspires awe and wonder, we will stop and admire the view. When a principle has an obvious life application, we will pause and try it on. Occasionally we will veer away and enter the deep, enchanted forests of unfathomable, eternal mysteries and offer possible explanations to help comprehend controversial or mind-boggling concepts. I want the reader to glean more than just the cold facts and formulas of Christianity; I want him or her to see its beauty, its wonder, and feel the awe of its cosmic impact.

This brings up a point on which I need the reader's tolerance and understanding. For a book of this kind to be complete and useful, it seems necessary to touch on these deep and controversial mysteries of the Faith — mysteries that no one can explain with utter confidence in his accuracy. Over the years my own views on many of these topics have changed, some more than once, and they may change again. What I have put in this book represents my best thinking at the moment of writing. Tomorrow I may wish I could change a paragraph or two to accommodate some new insight or discovery. In most cases where controversy reigns I have presented both sides of the view, though I admit, I generally weight the presentation toward my own bias. In doing so, I am speaking for nobody but myself. If your bias runs counter to mine, I hope you will not let our difference ruin the usefulness of the book for you. It's doubtful that you could find a book that treats these subjects in full agreement with you on every point. Please take what you can use and forgive the rest.

I have submitted this manuscript to a number of diverse readers that include preachers, theologians, students, and ordinary Christians. Among the many I have to thank for their input are Jim Bullock, Curtis Shelburne, David Langford, Dan Bouchelle, and Tim Ketchersid. I owe special thanks to four people: to Gene Shelburne and Lyndon Latham who invited me to fly to their city where they took a full day off so we could spend it using each others' minds as anvils on which to hammer out answers to many of the problem areas in this manuscript. Not only did they give me extremely valuable input, they gave me one of the most enjoyable days of my life; to my father Tommy Williams whose critique and contributions have improved the manuscript immensely; and to my wife Faye whose belief in this project from the outset has done much to encourage me to finish it.

Some readers may recognize the influence of familiar writers in these pages — writers such as C.S. Lewis, G.K. Chesterton, Major W. Ian Thomas, Francis Schaeffer, and George MacDonald. I gratefully acknowledge my debt to these great men, and I hope I have partially discharged it in the writing of this book. Thanks to these and other influences too subtle to recognize or too numerous to mention, this book now rests in your hands.

— T.M. Williams

1 The Being Before the Beginning

Imagine that nothing exists but black, cold, empty space. Imagine the universe as an empty void stretching endlessly in all directions without stars, planets, meteors, comets, sun, or earth — without a single atom of matter or a single pulse of energy. How could anything come to be in such a universe? Is it possible that existence could come about out of absolute nothing? Human reason says no; something cannot come out of nothing. The necessary alternative is that something had to exist always, but our minds stagger at the concept of anything or anyone existing that has no beginning. Both alternatives seem impossible, yet one of them must be true; either something existed always, or something came into existence out of nothing.

What we face when we consider beginnings is the fact that beginnings cannot be explained by the laws of nature. We can study nature to learn how existing things behave and reproduce, but not how they originally came to be. That is not a scientific question but a metaphysical one. Whether we believe in some sort of eternal self-existence or that existence began out of nothing, we are believing in a concept that is outside nature, or supernatural. We are forced to face the fact that there is something in beginnings beyond what the eye can observe, the mind can conceive, or science can explain.

Historically, most people have accepted the idea of God or a god who is self-existent and brought creation and life into being. Of course, we must admit that the idea of a self-existent God is just as much beyond human comprehension as self-existent matter or beginnings out of nothing.

To assume the existence of an eternal, supernatural God who created matter, energy, life, and intelligence is neither more scientific nor unscientific than to assume that these things are self-existent or came into being in an empty universe. The concept of God is not a matter of blind religious faith; it is a reasonable answer to a question that cannot be addressed scientifically. We believe in God not because we can prove beyond all possible doubt that he is there, but because no alternative conclusion fits the evidence as well as God does. Nothing else gives us a rational explanation for existence, life, energy, and intelligence.

What is God Like?

Why do we have to wonder about God? If there really is a God, why must he be so mysterious? Why can't he speak to us with a real voice and show himself face-to-face so we can know for certain that he is there and understand clearly what he 1 Timothy 6:16 wants from us? One answer is that God can't show himself to us directly because he is beyond our senses. We have no antennae that will pick up his signals, and even if we could, such supernatural data as a God would transmit would likely overload our mortal circuitry. The difference between our nature and his is too great for natural one-to-one communication.

You can visualize something of the problem by imagining how you would go about making yourself known to an earthworm. Attempting to explain yourself to an earthworm would not only look silly, it would be futile. If the worm has senses capable of picking up your voice at all, it would be as a meaningless noise, perhaps like rumbling thunder or the buzzing of a bee.

While we can understand most of the purpose and activities of earthworms, they can understand nothing about us. The higher can understand the lower but not vice versa. It is possible that an invisible God may be attempting to communicate with us continually in one way or another, and we may feel the effects of his activity at every moment without suspecting that he is the cause.

God does not show himself directly because we are not good enough to endure the intensity of his presence. As Shakespeare said, we are play actors who spend most of our waking lives on stage. We are always pretending to be better

14

than we are and trying to hide or excuse our faults and guilts. We lose our tempers, we ignore the needs of others, we lust, we are greedy, we break laws when it suits us, and we tell little fibs now and then to avoid unpleasant encounters or responsibilities. Then we downplay the seriousness of these faults and think God should give us high marks because we go to church regularly and don't pull the wings off flies. We wear our virtues like masks, thinking they will cover up the unsightly rash of sin that infects us; but it doesn't work. God sees through the mask. Those blemishes on our nature are clearly visible to him. We are neither pure enough nor real enough to present our true selves to him, and he is too pure and too real to present himself to a fake. If you were to show up at an important job interview wearing a Clark Gable or Marilyn Monroe mask hoping to impress the human resources director with your good looks, it would be impossible for him to take you seriously. We cannot expect God to take us seriously or speak to us face-to-face when we are wearing masks to hide the truth about ourselves.

No one has ever seen God face-to-face, but it is hardly possible to think of him without bringing up some sort of mental image. In childhood most of us start thinking of God as an old man with a long, white beard, probably because we associate eternal existence with old age. These first impressions are hard to erase. This is an erroneous concept, of course, but it is probably no worse than anything we might substitute for it. Any concept we have of God is sure to be as false as the concept a thinking earthworm would have of us. Whatever mental picture you have, it falls pitiably short of the truth. The majesty and glory of God is as much beyond imagination as his eternal existence.

Psalm 50:21

The Attributes of God

1 Samuel 2:3
1 Kings 8:39
Psalm 139:1-6
Isaiah 40:27,28

We are right to think of God as a person because he is a personal God. He is not some kind of vague, disembodied energy, or dreamy, distant, awakening consciousness of the universe. He is not an ambiguous type of *Star Wars* force, available for opportunistic villains or heroes to use for their own ends. God is not, as some Eastern religions would have us think, composed of everything in the universe. If God's being were dependent on the universe, he would cease to be when the universe finally runs down and burns out. The universe is not God or any part of God. He is separate from the universe just as a carpenter is separate from his house. God was God before the universe existed.

To say that God is personal does not mean that he actually has a body like ours. It means that he has a mind and will — he thinks and acts — but he is much more than a person as we understand personhood from our experience with fellow humans. God has qualities that place him above categories and beyond human comprehension. Let's briefly examine some of these known qualities one by one.

First, God is *eternal*, which means his life is without beginning or end. There was never a moment when he did not exist, and there will never be such a moment. He had no beginning and he will have no end. Once in our history, he called himself I AM, which means that he is always what he always is.

Second, God is *omnipotent*, (or *almighty* as some Bible translations put it). He is the source and controller of all the power in the universe. Nothing is impossible with God.

Most of us have played at challenging this assertion by coming up with proposed acts that seem impossible even for God. Some think they've got him stumped when they propose such problems as, "God can't make two plus two equal five," or, "God can't break a promise he has made." But impossibilities such as these are nonsensical. C.S. Lewis reasoned that an idea which makes no sense in its own right does not suddenly take on sense and become a possibility just because you add the words, "God can" to it. The name of God cannot be used as a magic incantation that brings sense out of silliness.

God certainly will not (or, if you insist, cannot) break a promise, because what he does must always be consistent with what he says, and both must be consistent with what he is. Who God is and what God does is the ultimate basis of truth. This is why the Bible tells us that God cannot lie (another thing that God cannot do). Saying that God could lie is nonsense in

Genesis 1:1
John 1:1-3

Isaiah 55:8,9

1 Chronicles
29:11,12

Deuteronomy 33:27
Psalm 135:13
Isaiah 40:28
Exodus 3:14

Matthew 19:26
Luke 1:37
Job 42:2

Hebrews 6:18

the same category as saying that two plus two can equal five. Two plus two cannot equal five because God, whose nature is order and consistency, has decreed that mathematics will be orderly and consistent. The universe itself survives only because it is based on orderly and consistent laws that hold it together — laws which flow from the nature of God. To ask for the laws of addition to be variable and produce different sums from the same column of figures is to ask for the nature of reality to change. If creation were not based on stable laws of mathematics, atomic equations would go out of kilter and the universe would collapse into chaotic meaninglessness. What God decrees is truth; anything that contradicts him is a lie. To say that God could cause two plus two to equal five is to say that the truth can be a lie. The words are meaningless nonsense. Nothing that goes against the nature of God is possible. What God is defines what *possible* means. Omnipotence means that everything possible at all is possible with God.

Psalms 139:8
Jeremiah 23:24
Acts 17:27

John 4:24

Third, God is *omnipresent*, which means that he is always everywhere. God is present with you at this moment, and simultaneously present on the bleak surface of an asteroid billions of light years away. We might assume that God's omnipresence means he is unthinkably huge, but size probably has nothing to do with it. God is a spirit, and his size is a mystery we cannot explore. The concept of size may mean nothing at all in relation to God. His presence encompasses all galaxies; yet he exists totally within the spaces between electrons, protons, and neutrons of the smallest atom. There is nowhere that God is not.

Proverbs 15:3
Matthew 10:29,30
Job 34:21,22
Hebrews 4:13
1 John 3:20

Fourth, God is *omniscient*. He knows all and sees all. The Bible tells us that he knows each time a sparrow falls to the ground. He also knows the exact count of the hairs that grow on your head, which is an incredible feat of accounting. The Bible does not give us this bit of theological trivia to make us think our hair is all that important; God just wants us to understand that nothing escapes his attention.

Psalms 147:5
Luke 1:37

Fifth, God is *infinite*. This is a sort of catch-all word that summarizes all we know of God. It means that he is not subject to any limitations at all.

Three Gods or One?

Genesis 1:26

There are places where the Bible reads as if God is speaking to someone even though no one else is present. The first chapter of Genesis quotes him as saying, "Let *us* make man, in *our* image, in *our* likeness." To whom was he talking? The New Testament answers by showing us that even when God is by himself, he is not alone. He is a unit of three individual personalities, or three distinct persons. The three are identified separately as the Father, the Son, and the Holy Spirit. All three are equal and all three are God. The word commonly used to express this three-in-one bond is *Trinity*.

Matthew 28:19
John 1:1-3
2 Corinthians 13:14
1 Peter 1:2

The true nature of the Trinity of God is, of course, beyond human understanding. We don't know how it is possible for three individual beings to form a single, unified being and yet retain their distinctness. However, we have a few types of unities in our world that may provide dim images to help us grasp the idea a little better. A marriage is made up of two altogether different people; yet in a sense that we all understand, the two are one. They have a completeness together that either lacks alone. A triangle is a triangle only when it has three separate, connecting sides. On the other hand, God is not like Three-in-One Oil. When the three oils that form this mixture are poured together, they lose their distinctness. When they become one, they are no longer three.

The three persons of God unite in such a way that the combination is like forming another being so complete and so individual that we address him by the singular personal pronoun *he* instead of the plural *they*. Yet none of the three sacrifices anything of his own uniqueness to the bond.

Genesis 1:3

Each of the three persons of God has his own special nature. The Bible shows God the Father to be the idea generator, the starter of things, the speaker. God the Son is the doer, the builder, the word that is spoken. The Son is the projection of the Father. He is the light ray from the flame that is God. The Bible defines the work of the Holy Spirit less clearly, but from the data we are given, we see him as the sustainer — the one who protects, directs, and keeps things running. He operates what the Father originates and the Son creates. He is the

John 1:1-5

Romans 8:11,14
John 16:7
Acts 16:6

heat wave from the flame that is God — the God you can feel.

Perhaps it would not be too far out of line to picture the Father as the architect; the Son as the builder; and the Holy Spirit as the operations manager. But there is no need for us to think of God as being divided up into thirds. He presents himself to us as the one God, and that is how we should relate to him. The activities of the three members of the Trinity seem to merge and flow into each other in ways that defy our attempts to sort them into neat, well-defined categories; and there is no need for us to trouble our minds trying. In spite of the complexities of God's nature, he presents himself to us simply as God.

The God Who Loves You

1 John 4:8

The one definition of God that we hear most often is that God is love. This definition is true and biblical, and it is also warm and comforting; but it is often misunderstood. God is love, of course; but it is easy to invert the equation and take it to mean that love is God. That is, since the principle of love is the highest we know, we enthrone it at the pinnacle of our values and treat it as our one absolute. If God and love are the same, then anything done in the name of love must be good. This principle is true if we define love properly, but it is often abused because we tend to redefine love according to what seems loving at the moment. This "seat-of-the-pants" concept of love is usually disastrous because it leads men and women to ignore the absolute commands of morality in favor of doing the thing that seems least painful or the thing that promises immediate happiness. The child who should get a paddling gets "Now, now; we shouldn't do that," instead because inflicting pain does not seem loving. The unmarried couple follow their passions into physical intimacy because, "It's okay if we truly love each other."

We could avoid the devastating consequences of such thinking if we were more wary of the misrepresentations of truth that keep popping up in pop religion. God is love, but the Bible also says he is a consuming fire, a king, and a judge. It also speaks of his wrath. None of these sterner descriptions of God

Deuteronomy 4:24
Romans 2:6-8
Ephesians 5:6

19

are inconsistent with his love. It is altogether loving for him to get angry and punish when he sees us behaving in ways that are self-destructive. Because he loves us, he burns us with a painful but purifying fire that cleans everything out of our lives that is not eternal.

God's love is not just a soft, warm feeling. He doesn't love us like a doting grandfather or an indulgent uncle, but with a tough love that wants the ultimate best for us even at the expense of our present comfort. Like a surgeon or a dentist, God will remove the fatal tumor or the abscessed tooth in spite of our screams of protest against the pain.

The God You Can Know

God does not speak to us face-to-face or in an audible voice, but he speaks to us in many ways that we can learn to recognize. He speaks through the speed limit sign we pass on the way to work or school. Such signs are the voice of his law which protect us from the unrestrained impulses of our fellow humans, as well as our own. God speaks through our supervisors or teachers as they assign the day's tasks. Through them he gives us ways to fit and function as contributors to society. God speaks when we see a distressed motorist standing by a car with a steaming radiator. He is calling us to give his care and concern to a fellow struggler.

Romans 13:1

God speaks to us through the Bible. In the Bible he gives us guidelines to make our behavior conform to the way we were designed to function. The Bible is a sort of manual for the care, upkeep, and operation of the human machine. It tells us how to keep thoughts in focus, speech oiled, and actions controlled so that your relationships with God and man will be happy and harmonious.

2 Timothy 3:16

God speaks through your conscience. In fact, the human conscience is one of the stronger evidences that God exists. Obviously, it is not a part of our reasoning processes because what it asks us to do is often not reasonable. It is not a part of human nature because it often asks us to do things we would not naturally do. The natural thing is to keep the ten dollar bill the clerk accidentally gives as change. The reasonable thing is

Romans 2:15
Romans 9:1
John 8:7-9

to tell a harmless lie about a broken fan belt to explain being late for work. But conscience — that persistent, intrusive, uninvited voice — steps in from somewhere beyond reason and beyond nature to urge us to do the opposite of the reasonable and natural. Conscience is a sort of closed-circuit speaker system God has beamed into our minds, and the voice we hear urging us to do the right thing is his. Of course, we can tune him out. Or we can learn to sneak our own thoughts through the speaker system, thus overriding God's voice with reasons why the thing we want to do is better than the thing we ought to do. Or we can ignore the speaker so much that in time, we no longer hear it; and finally, so much that God turns it off. But if untampered with, conscience is one of the most obvious — and often most troublesome — ways God has of speaking to us.

Hebrews 9:14

God sometimes speaks to us through circumstances. He will take away an apparently good opportunity in order to turn you toward one that is even better. He may thwart your own cherished plans in order to draw your attention to the plan your life was meant to follow.

Matthew 7:6
Luke 18:1
Ephesians 6:18
1 Thessalonians
5:17
Matthew 7:7-11

God talks to you in many ways, and he wants you to talk to him. He wants you to feel free to spill out your innermost feelings — your hopes, your wants, and even your doubts. There is no use pretending to God that you don't have doubts. The honest expression of doubt is one of the surest roads to faith; God will answer the honest questioner. As you learn to communicate with God, you will find that his presence becomes real in spite of his silence and invisibility. You can come to know him in a way that will leave no question in your mind that he is there and is personally concerned with you. And when you talk to him, he wants you to feel free to call him Father. Think of it: the eternal, omnipotent, omniscient, omnipresent, infinite master of the universe wants you to call him Daddy.

Romans 8:15

There was a time in human history when God was not inaudible or distant or hard for man to find. In fact, God did not intend for communication between himself and his creation to be strained or difficult as we now find it to be. Man was once comfortable with God and delighted to be in his presence. Communication with him was as easy and natural as with a close friend. In fact, it seems that the reason God created man was to have a being in the universe apart from himself who would voluntarily maintain an intimate relationship with him. How this relationship was established, lost, and regained is the story that unfolds in the rest of this book.

Questions for Discussion: Chapter 1

1. Why is the question of origins not a scientific one?

2. Which is the most reasonable and why? That matter and life come from nothing; that they are self-existent; that they were created.

3. Is God personal?

4. What do we mean by the term *Trinity*?

5. Are there limitations to God's omnipotence?

6. Is there any difference between the statements "God is love" and "love is God?

7. How does God communicate with us today?

2 The Beginning

When you take the tour of Carlsbad Caverns in New Mexico, the guide leads you to a certain place deep inside the winding corridors of the cave where he stops and turns out the lights. Suddenly you find yourself in a thick, black darkness you can almost feel. Absolutely nothing is visible in that darkness, and after a few moments it is easy to imagine that absolutely nothing exists. As you strain your eyes in a futile attempt to pick up a single dim ray out of the blackness, you begin to get an idea of what the emptiness of space was like before the beginning of the universe. No stars, no sun, no moon, no light of any kind relieved the oppressive weight of endless darkness. But there was no need for light because there was nothing to see. Matter did not exist — not a speck of dust or a single atom. The unrelenting blackness of space would have seemed hopelessly dead and barren to our senses, but it was not, for it was inhabited by the presence of the omnipotent God who was about to begin a spectacular project: the creation of the universe.

Genesis 1:1
Hebrews 1:10

At the dawn of prehistory, God bound together countless trillions of minute charges of energy to form the atomic structure we know as matter, the raw material from which he would build the universe. Some believers think this primeval creation could not have occurred much more than several thousand years ago, whereas others are convinced it must have happened a few million years ago. But there is no reliable way for us to pinpoint the event in time, and the Bible gives no clue.

In 1650 the Catholic theologian Archbishop Ussher calculated the date of creation to be 4004 B.C. He arrived at that particular date by working his way back through the many genealogies listed in the Bible. However, he made several assumptions. For example, he assumed that the original creation of the heavens and the earth as related in the first two verses of Genesis was included in the six days of creation described in the rest of the chapter. Such an assumption is unwarranted, as we can see by looking at the text:

1. In the beginning God created the heavens and the earth.
2. And the earth was formless and void, and darkness was over the surface of the deep; and the Spirit of God was moving over the surface of the waters.
3. Then God said, "Let there be light"; and there was light.

In verses one and two we have the original creation of matter and a description of its chaotic condition. In verse three we have God speaking light into existence, which initiates the first step in the shaping of matter into the forms of the universe as we know it. There is no hint as to how much time might have elapsed between verses two and three. The earth of verse two could have lain formless and empty for any amount of time before the creation of light in verse three began the six days of creation.

Too rigid an insistence on Ussher's chronology can lead to some desperate extremes in trying to defend the Bible. Some well-meaning Christians have even tried to explain away certain fossils by claiming they were pre-aged and planted in the appropriate geologic strata by God himself to confound man's arrogant search for knowledge. As a parallel they cite the creation of man and woman, who were also created in a "pre-aged" condition, appearing to be, say, twenty-one years old at the moment they were created. But the example is not really parallel to the claim. Man and woman were created in a perfect condition that reflected the epitome of vibrant life and health, which is a reflection of the nature of God. Fossils are the result of death and ruin and decay, which are foreign to the nature of God. To claim that God would deceive by such manipulation is to call God a liar. We are taught that creation reflects the nature of God, and God's nature does not include death, falsity or deception. This extreme argument is not followed by many Christians, even those who reject the vast ages claimed for the formation of the "geological column."

Psalm 19:1

What is important to note is that even Bible-believing scientists are not in total agreement over the age of the earth. The scientists of the Creation Research Society opt for a creation week no more than about 10,000-15,000 years ago. Authors Hugh Ross and John Clayton opt for longer ages, while still believing God to be in control. Of course, man's nature does include falsity and deception, and he is also prone to error. Perhaps the "experts" are wrong about the age of the earth. The fact that we cannot verify should make us cautious, not quick to jump in either direction at claims that do not square with our own preconceptions. There is a great need for care and openness as we study carefully just what the Bible does or does not actually say and what the fossils really do prove or disprove before we assume a conflict between the claims of science and the claims of the Bible. We, too, can be wrong when we try to draw conclusions too specific to be supported by the incompleteness of the evidence.

There is no need for Christians to insist absolutely on Ussher's chronology. The idea of a much older earth does not in itself actually clash with anything we can positively determine from Genesis. The first verse of Genesis tells us that God caused matter which had never existed before in any form to come into being out of sheer nothingness. The second verse describes the earth as a shapeless blob of water and mud. God may have purposely created the earth in this lump-like condition to serve as his supply of raw material to shape and mold as a sculptor models his clay. But some opt for another possibility: When God created the earth in verse one, he could have made it a perfectly formed and furnished sphere, complete with oceans, continents, weather, and even life. Then some cataclysmic disaster may have reduced it to the shapeless, empty condition of verse two. In the phrase, "And the earth was formless and void," the word for "was" in the original Hebrew text could alternatively be translated "had become." If the earth *had become* formless and void after having been created perfect, that original world could have been populated with animals, humans, human-like beings, or even other creatures that don't exist now. This theory could allow for some of the unexplained

Genesis 1:1

Genesis 1:2

27

bones and fossils that puzzle us today to be remains from this possible world before our world.

The Six Days of Creation

Whether the world was raw material or ruined material, God did not intend to leave it shapeless and empty. At a chosen moment in time, he towered above its watery surface, and his mighty voice thundered, "Let there be light;" and the universe was flooded with the brightness of the first morning.

Genesis 1:3

Genesis 1:6

Genesis 1:9-13
Psalm 95:5

Genesis 1:14-19

On the next day God covered the earth with a layer of fresh, clean air (called a *firmament* in some Bible translations) upon which he floated a layer of clouds. On the third day he commanded islands and continents to emerge from the depths of the water. Then, at his word, every kind of grass, trees, bushes, and other flora sprouted from the ground, covering the naked earth with a leafy, green coat. On the fourth day he placed the sun in command of the daytime sky. He made the moon and crowned her queen of the night, then sprinkled her sky with the twinkling glitter of millions of stars.

Some have noted that God created light on the first day, but did not create the sun, moon, and stars until the fourth day. Is there a discrepancy here? To answer, it seems that on the first day he created the concept of light — the activity of light rays emanating from energized objects and reflecting off of surfaces and onto sensitized retinas that can interpret form and color by them. Then on the fourth day he created the sun and stars that give us our light sources. He rounded up the light and contained it within these forms.

At the end of that fourth day, the earth was little like the world we know now. Everything was clean, fresh, and perfect. Healthy green plants grew everywhere, and the trees had no dead leaves or broken branches. Dazzling flowers bloomed extravagantly, and none of them bore thorns. You could walk barefoot across the grass without getting a sticker in your foot. Any fruit or vegetable you could possibly want grew freely and without the blight of worms or rot. The weather and climate were perpetually springlike — never too hot and never too cold. Sparkling dew bathed the mornings and gentle breezes cooled the evenings. There were no hailstorms, hurricanes, earthquakes, floods, or tornadoes. That fourth night fell on a perfect and beautiful new earth, but it was a still and silent earth. Nothing yet lived upon it that could enjoy its idyllic beauty and perfection.

Genesis 1:20-25
Then on the fifth and sixth mornings, the silence and still-ness gave way to a fantasy of sound and activity as God began to create animals. For the next two days he drew forms from his infinite imagination and soon had the earth crawling, hopping, fluttering, galloping, bleating, clucking, honking, braying, bark-ing, chattering, chirping, slithering, burrowing, and swimming with thousands of furry, feathery, and scaly creatures.

Romans 1:20
If you tend to think of God as a stern-faced killjoy who is above humor and lightheartedness, take a fresh look at some of these animals and you may see something about his nature that most people seem to miss. Look at the fireflies flickering across your lawn on a May evening. God didn't have to give that little beetle a built-in flashlight; he could have let it bump along in the dark like any other bug. Instead, he gave us a spontaneous light show to punctuate the evening concert of katydids. Listen to a mockingbird as it sits in a treetop and chirps away at an endless string of imitations. Would a straight-laced God have thought up such a delightful mimic? Look at an elephant's trunk, a giraffe's neck, a kangaroo's pocket, a penguin's suit, a raccoon's mask, a pelican's beak, a peacock's tail, and a zebra's stripes. The lavish and spectacular variety of color, form, sound, and infinite creativity is both awesome and delightful. There is no reason to think God enjoyed making these creatures any less than we enjoy having them share our world. Each animal shows us something about the kind of God we have — a God with a twinkle in his eye: a God of boundless inventiveness who delights in colors, forms, textures, and sounds.

Psalm 8
Psalm 19:1-6
Psalm 148
We get immune to things that are common to us and fail to see their inherent wonder. We hardly notice the towering majesty of a golden column of cumulus clouds; the dazzling dance of a field of buttercups; the cheerful gurgle and sparkle of a rushing stream; or the soothing, rhythmic patter of a spring shower. But had we lived our entire lives on the dead, gray

plains of the moon and found ourselves suddenly set down in the midst of such sounds and colors, we would think were in a wild and incredible fantasy land. The main reason so many readers enjoy books of fantasy and science fiction is that such stories renew the wonder that things are as they are. When readers enter by imagination into a creative author's alternative world, they realize that the real world in which they live is also the product of a rich imagination.

G.K. Chesterton pointed out that things are not as they are because they are merely natural (by which we often mean commonplace or random), but because a creator *decided* that they would be as they are. As far as we know, God could have made the grass purple or had porcupines growing on pineapple trees. Gravity could have been engineered to pull masses sideways instead of downward so that we would all have to live standing horizontally on the south sides of mountains. We might imagine, with wonder and delight, a fantastic world of flying flowers, when all we need to do is look in our own backyards to see real butterflies. It is just as much a wonder that water is sometimes liquid, sometimes solid, and sometimes vaporous as it would be if granite stones behaved the same way. We are fascinated by the novelty of Tolkien's walking trees as if it were less a wonder that our world has walking men and women. On the Greeks' mythical Mount Olympus, nectar flowed like water. In our world water flows like water, and had we just arrived from the bone-dry surface of the moon, the marvel of that fact would make us think we were in Alice's wonderland. Our home planet is the most spectacular of fantasy lands if we can only manage to keep the creeping blahs of familiarity from lulling our wonder to sleep.

The Clockwork Creation

Romans 1:20

Job 39:1-30

The animals God created show us something else about him that we need to notice; they show him as the ultimate engineer. Again, because creation has become so commonplace to us, we fail to appreciate how intricate and complex is the design of the most lowly and common creatures of nature. Had modern engineers designed and constructed a single grasshopper that functions as efficiently as the billions that come and go from the earth each summer, the feat would merit a Nobel Prize. In fact, it would be the greatest single engineering accomplishment in the history of civilization. A grasshopper is a self-contained machine that walks, flies, jumps, sees, hears, feels, avoids danger and has some degree of awareness. It finds, takes on, and processes its own fuel, and reproduces itself. All this takes place in a compact, miniature body often less than one inch long. Nothing man has created comes close to rivaling the functional efficiency of the grasshopper or the millions of other living species that share our planet.

God designed each of these creatures to fill a specific role. Each is programmed with a set of built-in instructions that tell it exactly how to do the job for which it was designed. A garden spider has a sort of built-in computer that is programmed to spin giant orb webs. The spider does not need to spend any time thinking out the construction pattern of her web, because the built-in program contains all the data she needs to spin it perfectly. Bees make their honeycombs automatically, without forethought or blueprint, and they make them exactly right, every time, on the first try. They don't need practice or apprenticeship to learn the honeycomb trade. They emerge from the egg with a prerecorded program that tells them all they will ever need to know about making honeycombs.

These built-in programs cannot be changed. A bee can never be trained to make the cells of its honeycomb triangular instead of hexagonal. There are no Picasso spiders or Caruso canaries. You will never find a spider rebelling against the old-fashioned, standard orb-patterned web of its parents and spinning a contemporary, free-form web embellished with touches of avant-garde creativity. No canary ever ventures into some aviary equivalent of atonal or experimental music, but sticks to the classical repertoire of its ancestors. It cannot change its tune or increase its range. The behavior of all animals is permanently set and limited by their own preprogrammed instructions. We call these instructions *instinct*.

Instinct exercises much more control over the lower animals than the higher. A butterfly is programmed completely as it is formed within the cocoon. At the moment it emerges, it has stored within all the information to guide its function that it will ever have. A dog has more intelligence than a butterfly and therefore less need of instinct. But while the dog's brain has considerable storage capacity for learned behavior, its basic behavior is still programmed. Dogs can learn to shake hands and play frisbee, but they still do the same doggy things their ancestors have done throughout canine history; they are territorial, they attach themselves to humans, they bark, chase cats, and howl when you sing *Auld Lang Syne*. Greater intelligence gives the higher animals more optional behavior than the lower, but ultimately, instinct controls them all.

Genesis 1:25

At this point in the six days of creation, everything worked like a clock. Nothing was out of kilter; everything functioned perfectly as designed. All the animals were programmed to fit in perfect harmony with their perfect world. But God was about to take a tremendous risk and embark upon a grand experiment. He was about to make a creature that would not be controlled by instinct — a creature that would be free to act as it chose. The stage was now set for the crowning act of God's creation.

Questions for Discussion: Chapter 2

1. Explain why the creation of the heavens and the earth is separate from the six days of creation.

2. Discuss what fossils can or can't tell us about the date of creation.

3. Could things have been created differently than they appear now?

4. What does creation show about the nature of God?

5. What do you think is the purpose of animals?

6. Why do you think animal behavior is limited by instinct?

3 The Creature with a Spirit

Like the claim in the king's song from Lerner and Loewe's *Camelot*, there was one, brief, shining moment when things were exactly as they should have been. For an all-too-short span of time, Paradise, Arcadia, Utopia, Camelot, Shangri-La, El Dorado, Atlantis existed. At the end of the sixth day of creation, the kind of perfect world men and women dream of was a reality.

As we read in the previous chapter, God began the sixth day of creation by making the animals. Before the day was over he embarked on the crowning act of his creation. He took a few handfuls of dirt and molded it into that familiar shape that we adore in the mirror. He created man in the general fashion of a mammal, but with several important differences: He made man to stand upright, gave him versatile hands with opposing thumbs, installed a larger, much more complex and analytical brain, and endowed him with the power of reason and speech.

In addition to his mammal-like body, the new-formed man had two other components that made up his total being: a soul and a spirit.* Unlike the body, the soul and the spirit are invisible. The soul of man has a function much like the instrument panel of an airplane; it is the control center of his behavior. The soul is where the levers, switches, warning lights, and buttons of the nerves, senses, and muscles are located.

Genesis 1:26,27

1 Thessalonians 5:23

Hebrews 4:12

Genesis 2:7

---

*Some may question the use of the word *soul* here. Many think the word is a synonym for the word *spirit*. The Bible does indeed sometimes seem to use the two words interchangeably. In the account of the death of Rachel in Genesis 35:18: ". . . as her soul was departing . . ." the term *soul* may refer to her spirit. But the incisiveness of the Word of God is described in Hebrews 4:12 as being ". . . sharper than any two-edged sword, piercing even to the division of soul and spirit . . ." In this passage, soul clearly does not mean the same as spirit. For consistency and clarity, the terms are not used interchangeably in this book. The term "soul" is always used in the sense defined in this chapter.

The soul has three sub-components by which it controls the body. These are the mind, the emotions, and the will. The mind is man's thinking and formulating organ. It computes and analyzes the data fed to it through the body's senses and fashions beliefs and conclusions based on this data. The mind is like the old *Star Trek*'s Mr. Spock — factual, analytical, and emotionless. The second part of the soul, the emotions, are the feelings generated by the data from the senses. The emotions include such feelings as affection, anger, sadness, and happiness. The third part of the soul is the will. The will takes the data passed on from the mind along with the feelings generated by the emotions and digests them to determine what the body wants to do. It tries to form a consensus from all the input it gets from the body through the mind and emotions. When the urgings of the emotions conflict with the analysis of the mind, the will usually accedes to whichever is stronger at the moment. The will is the "want to" element in man. It digests all the available data to determine the desires and preferences of the person.

Having a soul does not make man unique, because the higher animals, at least, also have souls. Every creature that moves about must have some sort of control center. If they don't actually have minds as we define minds, they have something more or less like minds that enable them to sort out and codify the information they get from their senses. And the higher animals, at least, have emotions, as we know from the growl of a dog or the purr of a kitten. They also have something like wills, or at least a mechanism by which the motivation to act emerges based on input from the senses, emotions, and mind, and determines whether they will fight or run, obey or ignore your call, gnaw on a bone or nap in the sun. In most cases animal instinct provides the impulse to act (though instinct can be overridden by conditioning). There is hardly any real choice involved. The will in animals is little more than a gate through which urgings come from the body and soul.

Job 32:8
James 2:26
Ecclesiastes 12:7

It is the third part of man that sets him apart from the animals and makes him truly unique. The difference is in what is at the control center. Instead of giving man a preprogrammed computer (instinct) to guide his behavior, God gave him a *spirit*. The spirit was designed to be the authority in the pilot's seat, providing the direction, the guiding principles, and the decision-making function for the body and soul. When the will arrives at its consensus — what the mind and emotion want to do — it passes it on to the spirit for a decision to act. Think of the mind, emotions, and senses as members of a sort of trade union. The will is the president of the union. It takes a vote to determine what the organism wants to do. It presents its petition — the results of the vote — to management, the spirit, for a decision. When the decision is made, the will goes back to the body and controls and disciplines it to conform to the decision of the spirit, sometimes overriding the pull of the senses

Matthew 26:41   and emotions. Or it may rebel against the directives of the spirit and let the mind or emotions have their way with the body.

In today's world, the process works something like this: A part of the body reacts to stimuli; let's say the nose smells a hamburger cooking. The emotions take the aromatic data from the nose and visualize the happiness and pleasure the body would receive if the burger were to be eaten. The mind analyzes the same aromatic data and concludes that food is available. It does a quick check on the status of the stomach and notes that it is not totally empty but could handle the burger. It does a check on the status of the body's finances and notes that funds are available to purchase the burger. The mind also notes that the body is several pounds overweight and that the spirit had previously issued a directive to limit food intake. The mind passes this information on to the will then steps away and the will takes over. The will tabulates the urging of the emotions and the analytical data from the mind and tells the spirit, "We want a hamburger." The spirit must decide whether to override its previous directive to limit intake and go with the urging of the will, or to abide by the directive and walk on by.

Man's spirit is significantly different from animal instinct. Animal instinct is automatic; it has no capacity for moral choice. Man's spirit is capable of making moral choices. It is also designed to be eternal. The spirit is the central self, the seat of self-awareness. It is in your spirit that you know you are yourself. The most significant difference between animal instinct and the human spirit is in its designed purpose. You might say that God made man's spirit hollow, or cup-shaped. Of course, the spirit is invisible and (to the best of our understanding) has no actual form. But to describe it as cup-shaped suggests the idea that it is meant to be a container; it is not complete within itself. We might just as easily say that man's spirit is like a candle, created to be the bearer of light.

1 Corinthians 3:16

Genesis 2:7

Ephesians 3:16

As God finished making this new creature with the cup-shaped spirit, he did an astonishing thing: He breathed his own life into the man. He filled the cup. He lit the candle from his own flame. He designed man to be a visible, physical container for the invisible Spirit of God. As the crowning touch to all creation, God filled man's cup-shaped spirit with his own Holy Spirit, giving man a special connection with God that no other creature had. In the place where the animals had instinct, the newly created man had God himself. Instead of responding machine-like to the coded impulses of a prerecorded program, the new man received live information directly from the mind of God. God's Spirit lived in man's spirit like the pilot on an airliner and conducted his affairs on earth by charting the direction of the man's mind, emotions, and will. Man was a living container for the life of God. He was the Creator's special representative to creation, designed to show by his own activity what God is like.

Genesis 2:20-25

God created mankind in two complementary models: male and female. Just as the polarity of a magnet reflects the polarity of the earth's gravitation, the two sexes were designed as living representatives of two powerful, interacting principles of nature. The male reflects the active, generative, initiating principle which we call masculine; the female reflects the responsive, nurturing, receptive, stabilizing principle we call feminine. Everything about the two sexes — shape, size, voice, features, organs, mental tendencies, and emotional responses — was designed to emphasize their differing roles. Where one is weak, the other is strong; what one is lacking, the other supplies. At the moment of creation these differences were

38

infused into the nature of the two in order to reflect the ebb and flow of mutual dependency in creation, and to draw them toward each other for mutual fulfillment and completeness.

Genesis 1:27

The two sexes also had the privilege of reflecting two very different aspects of the nature of God. God as the creator, the initiator, the actor, the protector and the defender of his creation is characterized as masculine. The male is designed to reflect this side of God's nature more suitably than the female. Yet there is another side of God, equally important and ex-

Isaiah 40:11

Hosea 11:3,4

tremely powerful. He is nurturing and responsive to the needs of mankind. He is tender and loving, gentle and empathetic. These feminine attributes of God are beautifully reflected in the design and function of the female. Of course, masculine and feminine traits overlap in the male and female just as they are both combined within the nature of God. Yet creation clearly shows us that the two sexes have unalterable attributes appropriate to their design.

In explaining why God created Adam before Eve, one little girl said, "First God made man. When he looked at what he had done he said, 'I think I can do better than that.' Then he made woman."

Genesis 2:8

The first man was named Adam; his wife was named Eve. God gave the newlywed couple a beautiful, park-like garden home called Eden, where they began a blissful honeymoon in a perfect new world.

The Choice

You may question whether the control-by-Spirit design of the man and woman was a real improvement over the control-by-instinct design of the animals. What does it matter whether a creature is governed by God or by instinct? Either way he is still governed. One way seems to make him a puppet; and the other a robot. Neither seems to give him any say in his own behavior.

It is true that the animals have no choice but to behave as they are made to behave. As we noted in the previous chapter, they cannot change their basic programmed modes of behavior. Fortunately, they do not have the capacity to want to change;

they are created content to be what they are. Adam and Eve, however, did have a choice. Even though they were made specifically to be containers for the life of God, they were not forced into accepting that role. God did not twist their arms. He did not invade their lives against their wills or compel their obedience in any way. He was not a landlord, but a guest. He lived in them by invitation only, and would get out of their lives the moment he was no longer welcome. As Calvin Miller has written, "Birds praise God by the beat of their wings; but man praises him by choice." God created man to be the creature in the universe who would show his greatness by more than merely functioning according to a pre-set program. Man would display the nature of God because he willingly chose to do so. Adam and Eve were not puppets; they were utterly free to accept or reject God's Spirit as the guiding hand at the control centers of their lives.

Genesis 2:8-17

God even made it easy for them to choose. There was no fine-printed contract; no long-term lease; no sacred vow; no oath signed in blood. God simply planted a tree in the middle of their garden and told them to leave it alone, because eating its fruit would bring in the evil twins pain and death to ravage and waste their perfect world. Getting God out of their lives would be easy; all they had to do was take a bite of that forbidden fruit. When they broke this one rule, God would know that he was no longer welcome. At that point he would get out like an evicted tenant and let evil and death move in.

A Perfect World

Evil and death: Adam and Eve did not know the meaning of the words nor the threat they posed to their way of life. Eden was a paradise of luxuriant, abundant life — a flawless world brimming with goodness and joy. These happy honeymooners had it made. Their superb, flawless bodies glowed with the sheen of perpetual health — no flu, no toothache, not even a sniffle. The environment of the new earth suited them so perfectly that they needed neither clothing nor artificial shelter.

Genesis 2:25

And their nakedness did not make them feel immodest or self-conscious in the presence of each other. They appreciated creation so acutely that their senses were not dulled by overexposure to the specialness of their differences. Their wills, voluntarily directed by God's Spirit, controlled their appetites and senses so perfectly that unmanaged desire was never a problem. Sexual desire was present, of course; even in Eden.

Genesis 1:28

God had told them to be fruitful and multiply. And the pleasure of satisfying these desires was certainly at least as sensational for them as for humans today. But unlike the wills we have today, the wills of Adam and Eve were able to control all appetites perfectly because of their solid link with the Spirit of God. Instead of being agitated beyond control by rampant, unharnessed senses, they happily obeyed the God who led them only into joy.

Adam and Eve never fought or argued because they were in perfect harmony with God and thus with each other. They never looked or felt a day older than the moment they were created, because God designed them to live forever in perfect health and without declining strength.

Genesis 1:26-28

Although Adam and Eve lived in a world of unimaginable beauty and harmony, their lives were not to be all fun and frolic. Humans are designed to be movers and shakers. They were created for significant activity, and all humans must feel this sense of significance for their lives to have meaning. Adam and Eve were given crucial responsibilities and tasks. As the six days of creation drew to a close, God crowned the new man and woman king and queen of the earth and gave them all its creatures as willing subjects. When Adam and Eve walked through Eden, creatures looked at them and saw the image of God, because God himself lived in their cup-shaped spirits. The royal couple was blissfully happy, as creatures always are when they function as designed.

Communication with God was not difficult for Adam and Eve. God was neither invisible nor inaudible to them as he is to us. He presented himself to them in a mode that they could

Genesis 3:8

hear and apparently see, for we are told that "he was walking in the garden in the cool of the day." The picture we get is that every evening God would drop by and the three of them would take a stroll through the garden, chatting as friends as they ambled along flower-lined paths and enjoyed the fresh beauty of creation.

This easy, unashamed, unself-conscious, intimate, face-to-face relationship with God was certainly the greatest delight in the lives of the first couple. But there came an ill-fated day when one simple but terrible deed sundered man and woman from God and stunned all creation with a devastating blow from which the universe has not yet recovered.

Questions for Discussion: Chapter 3

1. What are the three parts of man's soul?

2. What does man have instead of animal instinct?

3. Some have taught that sex is original sin. Is this true?

4. What did it mean for Adam to rule the earth and have dominion over it?

5. When man is controlled by God's Spirit, is he God's slave?

6. Is work a curse to mankind?

7. Did Adam and Eve pray?

4 The Creature Rebels

It has been reported that in 1904, there were only two automobiles in the entire state of Ohio. Although these two cars had over 41,000 traffic-free square miles to chug around in, they ended up colliding with each other. The fact that a calamity is highly unlikely is not enough to keep it from happening. Indeed, it often seems that some mysterious, mischievous, even malevolent force lurks in every plan, tripping, blocking, puncturing, breaking, spilling, ripping, and pushing things toward confusion and disorder. This persistent tendency is summed up in the famous maxim we know as Murphy's Law: If anything can go wrong, it will.

But you would think it hardly possible that things could go wrong in Eden. The perfect human couple in a perfect new world should have been virtually immune to disaster. Of course, evil was there for them to choose, but it was dormant. Like a radioactive contaminant stored in capsules and isolated with warning signs, evil was, so to speak, locked into the fruit of a particular tree; its deadly power rendered utterly harmless as long as it was left alone. To Adam and Eve, evil was merely a theoretical possibility in a world of active, rampant, overwhelming good. For them even to consider releasing evil from its fruit capsule seems so brazenly outrageous as to be unthinkable. It should have been easy for Adam and Eve to ignore that one, forbidden tree among a forest of others from which they could freely eat; but even in paradise, the thing forbidden became the thing desired. God's warning to avoid the tree was like a wet paint sign irresistibly drawing the touch of curious fingers. Murphy's Law got its grip on our race right there in Eden, and in this chapter we will see how it happened.

The Enemy

Genesis 3:1

As Adam and Eve worked and frolicked in their happy paradise, hostile eyes followed every move they made. The creature that watched was not one of the animals God made in the six days of creation; he came from some distant, shadowy past that we know nothing about. His name is Satan.

Who is Satan? Where did he come from? When and why did God create him? What was he doing in Eden? These are questions that no one can answer with authority. Most Christians believe he was once a chief angel in heaven who rebelled and was thrown out after waging war for the throne of God. This theory comes to us partly from John Milton's epic poem, *Paradise Lost*, and partly from the conclusions of theologians who have interpreted and connected certain passages in the

Isaiah 14:3-21

Revelation 12:1-17

books of Isaiah and Revelation. However, not all theologians accept the assumption that the Isaiah passage refers to Satan at all (Isaiah 14:4 tells us the passage is directed to the king of Babylon), or that the Revelation passage describes an angelic rebellion that occurred before Eden was created. There are serious problems with the chronology when one tries to place the war in heaven outlined in Revelation 12 before the creation of Man in Genesis 1. The truth is, we have more questions about Satan than we have answers, and his origin is a tantalizing mystery that simply is not revealed.

John 8:44

1 Peter 5:8

1 John 3:8

What we do know with certainty about Satan is this: he is utterly evil, and he hates man bitterly. How did Satan get such an evil nature? If he did rebel against God, why did he do it? Why does he hate man so intensely? The best we can do is follow these questions marks with "perhapses." Perhaps Satan held an ancient grudge against God and turned his fury on God's creation in revenge. Perhaps he was jealous that God had crowned Adam king of the earth instead of him. Perhaps he had lost a kingdom or some great position of his own, and was determined to steal Adam's kingdom to regain his lost glory. Perhaps he had been lord of the earth before it became the formless blob of Genesis 1:2. The true reason for Satan's evil and hate may be altogether different from any of these guesses, or it may even be that the popularly believed Miltonian theory is indeed true.

True or not, the theory that Satan is a rebel angel who was driven out of heaven is useful for two reasons: First, it does give us an explanation for his character that is consistent with what we know of him. Second, the theory puts good and evil in proper relationship to each other.

The Nature of Evil

Some religions teach that good and evil are equal opposites. *Dualism* is the concept that there are two equally powerful forces in the universe; one good and one evil. These two powers are engaged in a titanic struggle for dominance, and thus keep each other in check. Neither is the absolute standard for morality. Whether your actions are right or wrong depends on which of these powers claims your allegiance. Stealing a car would be a violation of principles if you are on the side of good, but perfectly acceptable behavior if you choose to align with the evil power.

Pantheism claims that good and evil are opposite sides of the same coin. According to this doctrine, you can hardly do any kind of good without at the same time doing some kind of evil. Cutting down a tree to build a house to shelter a family is good for the family but bad for the tree. A Sunday feast of roast beef is good for the diners but bad for some cow. An operation to remove a cancerous tumor is good for the patient but bad for the cancer cells. Just as electricity must have both a positive and negative charge, the universe must have the equalizing balance of both good and bad, joy and sorrow, pleasure and pain, kindness and cruelty, health and sickness, love and hate, life and death. Like a tightrope cyclist carrying a balancing pole, the universe must carry these equalizing pairs of opposites to keep itself in balance.

Genesis 1:31

But Christianity teaches that good and evil are neither equal nor opposite. It teaches that good is the nature of all original creation, and that evil is nothing more than a corruption of good. Good is the absolute standard of the universe and evil is merely a deviation from that standard. Good is the rule and evil is the infraction. This is where the idea of Satan as a fallen angel, whether true or not, gives a vivid picture that helps us see the nature of truth. God is the ultimate power in the universe and the source of all good. He made the universe good and intended that it remain that way. Satan is merely a created being, originally subject to God, but he grew proud and rebelled against God and the goodness of creation. His rebellion set up a reaction against good and brought in pride, hate, spite, envy, and lust; none of which exists as true opposites to good, but merely as reactors to it.

Our own experience shows us clearly which of these ideas about good and evil fits reality. If good and evil were equal opposites, it should be possible for us to want evil for its own sake just as we want good for its own sake. Doing or receiving evil should fulfill some need in us just as doing or receiving good does. But we all know that this is not the case. We help others, we love, we tell the truth, we work, we obey law because we expect the results of such behavior to be rewarding and satisfying. We do good and hope to receive good of some sort in return (even if it is only the comfort of knowing we did the right thing). But when we do evil, it is not because we hope to receive evil in return. We don't steal because we hope someone will turn around and steal from us. No one ever murdered because he looked forward to the agony of his guilt or because he hoped that someone would return the favor and thrust a knife into his own heart. We commit our evil acts because we think they are shortcuts to getting some sort of good or avoiding some sort of bad. We lie to deflect an uncomfortable or incriminating situation, not because we hope someone will lie to us. The thief steals money in the hope that he can buy something with it that will bring him happiness. The glutton eats more than he needs, not because he desires the health problems associated with obesity, but because he enjoys the good taste of food and the satisfaction of feeling full. We all commit our evil deeds hoping they will result in good consequences for us, not because we hope to receive evil in return. Whether we commit good or evil acts, the purpose is the same: to receive something that we think is good for us in some way — something that will give us good feelings or accomplish a good purpose.

These experiences show us that we cannot desire pain and

anguish in the same way that we desire joy and happiness. Good and evil are not equals. Good, or something we think will be good in the sense that it is desirable, fulfilling, protective, or satisfying is always our ultimate desire and evil is merely a perverted shortcut by which we think we can get to it. Evil is never done for its own sake; it never stands as an equal and opposite alternative to good. The difference between good and evil is not like the difference between white and black; it is like the difference between metal and rust.

The Attack

From the moment man and woman appeared in Eden, Satan began to plot their destruction. Why did God allow Satan into Eden? He certainly knew that Satan was there, and that his purpose was to wreck and ruin. Why didn't God protect his perfect new world by throwing out the evil intruder and locking the gate? Why did he tolerate an evil creature with destructive intent to be present in the midst of the good that he created?

As we explained in the previous chapter, God made Adam and Eve because he wanted free creatures in the universe who would choose voluntarily to reflect his nature. And for freedom to be authentic, there must be a choice. Freedom without options is meaningless. If God had made Adam and Eve free to choose but allowed them no options, it would have been as Henry Ford said when offering the first automobiles he manufactured: "You can have any color as long as it is black." It would be nonsense for God to tell Adam and Eve to be good if there were no possibility of their being bad. God gave them the option when he planted the tree of the forbidden fruit. Satan was powerless to harm them unless they exercised that option. Of course, Satan entered Eden with the intent of undermining their resolve and getting them to taste the fruit. The question was, would he succeed? In the name of freedom, God had to let that question be answered. Satan's presence in paradise would test whether or not the man and his mate would voluntarily choose to fill the role their creator fitted them for.

Genesis 3:1-5

2 Corinthians 11:14

On a day when Adam and Eve were apparently working in separate parts of Eden, Satan came into the garden in the form

49

of a serpent (which was an attractive creature in the beginning). Finding Eve alone, he approached the innocent queen and began the world's first religious argument. Armed with a poisonous mixture of barefaced lies and twisted truth, Satan hoped to cause Eve to question the rightness of God's arrangement for Adam and herself. He told her that God was holding back on them. They were not nearly as happy or powerful as they could be, because God was hiding mysterious wisdom that would broaden their horizons beyond imagination. Satan told Eve that a bite of that forbidden fruit would not kill her, as God had said; instead it would reveal marvelous secrets known only to the mind of God — secrets like the meaning of good and evil. Satan hinted that God had told them not to eat of the fruit because doing so would make them equal to him, and he did not want rivals in his universe.

Satan was telling Eve things so near the truth that they must have sounded very much like the truth. But in her perfect world she had never encountered deception and did not recognize its deadly face. She set aside what God had told her about the fruit, which left her soul as naked as her body. Ignoring God's warning left her defenseless as lies artfully clothed in the language of truth stepped easily through the open door of her mind.

The words that oozed from Satan's lips had the shape of truth but not the substance. They were venomous lies handsomely packaged in the language of reason and common sense. He didn't mean exactly what he knew she heard him say. It was true that Adam and Eve were meant to be like gods; they were made to be containers for the very Spirit of God. But Satan scored a hit when he pointed to the fruit that God would not let them eat and declared that it was not like a god to submit to a rule. How could they claim to be like God as long as he ordered and they obeyed? Gods are supposed to give the orders, not follow them. Satan urged Eve to get out from under God's thumb and do her own thing in her own way. Why should she sit meekly by and let anyone tell her what to do? She should break free of arbitrary rules imposed on her by others so she could find out what is right for herself. She should be free to become her own person and find her own self-fulfillment.

As Eve listened to that smooth-talking serpent, she looked at that bright, juicy fruit hanging there so easily within her reach. Her mouth began to water and her mind began to wonder whether that snake wasn't making pretty good sense. What could be wrong with learning the mysteries of good and evil? What could be wrong with being as wise as God? Why shouldn't she be free to live her own life in her own way? The more she thought, the more she doubted, and the more she doubted, the tastier that fruit looked. Finally, she reached out, grasped the fruit, pulled it from the tree, and bit deeply into it. It was delicious. She ran to find Adam.

Genesis 3:6

Adam must have been stunned to see the half-eaten fruit in his wife's extended hand. But when she held the fruit to his face and offered him the same choice Satan had offered her, Adam was not tempted. Whereas the scent of the forbidden fruit had been to Eve as the aroma of the gods, Adam smelled only the stench of death. He clearly understood that this cherished companion of his had just eaten her doom. We can imagine what he must have thought: "Death will now separate us and I will never see her again. She has been with me only for a short time, but already I wonder whether I can stand to live without her. God will provide for me in some way, of course; but what about her? Can I bear to leave her to face death alone? Perhaps if I sin along with her, God will find a way to pull us both out of death." Knowing fully well what he was doing, Adam deliberately received the fruit from his wife's extended hand and took the fatal bite. To him the taste must have been intensely bitter.

1 Timothy 2:14

The Fall

1 John 3:24

When Adam and Eve bit into that fruit, God's Spirit immediately vacated their lives. By disobeying this one rule, they showed God that they no longer wanted his direction, so he simply left. Now they were on their own. They had no one to answer to — no one to tell them what to do or when to do it. Never again would they willingly say, "God's will be done."

From now on it was to be, "I want what I want when I want it."

Jeremiah 10:23
Proverbs 1:28-31

However, there was a problem they had not anticipated. They were now free to do exactly as they pleased, but they found, to their surprise and dismay, that making things work their way was not at all easy. When God left Adam and Eve, he left them empty. He took his Spirit out of their cup-shaped spirits, but nothing moved in to take his place. When God bailed out, the pilot's seat was left vacant. If Adam and Eve had been animals, they could have let their built-in instincts take over like the captain of an airliner switching to automatic pilot. But they were not animals, and they had no such backup system. It was God's Spirit or nothing. And without his Spirit they were like an airliner flying with no pilot at all; they were completely out of control and headed for certain disaster.

Romans 7:18-23

As long as Adam and Eve had God in their lives, they were able to control themselves and nature perfectly. But without God, nature took control of them. With God they wanted only what they needed when they needed it. But without God they wanted whatever happened to look or feel good to them at the moment. The human will under the direction of the Spirit had been able to maintain total mastery of the senses. But with the Spirit gone, the flow of power reversed. When nature stimulated Adam's senses, his senses aroused his appetites. His appetites then demanded satisfaction from his will, and his will demanded that his spirit not stand in the way, and without God, his spirit was like a jellyfish — spineless and too weak to resist. It surrendered without a fight and said to the will, "You're too much for me to handle — just go on and do whatever you and the body want." And the will did just that.

Ecclesiastes 6:7

Things were the same for Eve. Her belly uncontrollably craved anything her eyes found appealing. Her feet obligingly took her to where her hands could grab the tempting morsel and stuff it into her mouth. Her will had no say in such matters because the control center from which the will should have been directed was empty. All the appetites of the body ran wild. Simple wishes swelled into wild ambitions; hungers into cravings; desires into lusts; and wants into demands because Adam and Eve had kicked out the only power capable of keeping these impulses in check. They thought that rejecting God's authority would bring them freedom, but instead they found themselves slaves to their own rampant and voracious appetites.

And to make matters worse, when Adam and Eve disobeyed God they gave Satan the foothold on the earth that he was looking for. We will explore how he took advantage of that victory in the next chapter.

Questions for Discussion: Chapter 4

1. Who is Satan? Where did he come from?

2. What is the difference between the Christian and the pantheistic view of evil?

3. Why did God allow Satan in Eden?

4. What did Satan mean when he told Eve she would be like God? How does this differ from authentic godlikeness?

5. Was Adam deceived by Eve into eating the forbidden fruit? Why did he do it?

6. How did Adam and Eve's relationship with God change after the fall?

5 The Grip of Sin and Death

After Adam and Eve disobeyed God by eating the forbidden fruit (the event known as the Fall), they found themselves at odds with God. Their rebellion against his will had left them with attitudes that were out of harmony with the universe, making them dangerous misfits in God's creation. They had decided to play their own made-up tune instead of following the conductor with the rest of the orchestra. They were made to be like God, but now they were not like God. They were created for the very purpose of bearing the life of God, but they had thrown God out. They were no longer useful in creation, for they had chosen not to fulfill the very purpose for which they were created.

1 John 3:4
1 John 5:17
James 4:17

The godless condition Adam and Eve experienced after the Fall is known as sin. Sin is nothing more nor less than failure to be like God. It is rejecting the law and order of the universe in favor of individual anarchy. It is refusing to obey stoplights, center stripes, and speed limits; insisting instead on driving just the way one wants. Sin goes much deeper than a simple act of disobedience; it is refusing to be what we were created to be, and refusing to recognize God as our authority.

2 Peter 2:1-3
Proverbs 14:12

We can see the sin of Adam and Eve reverberating in the lives of men and women today. Many mindsets that are absolutely wrong are applauded as desirable credos for living. Rampant individualism is admired. Pushing against limits is deemed good; limits are made to be broken ("Color outside the boundaries"). Resistance to authority is expected. Individual rights is the paramount virtue, even if it means killing unborn children and divorcing at will to keep from being boxed in by lifestyle-limiting responsibility. Every urge should be gratified: if you want it you should have it — which leads to runaway consumerism and unrestrained moral license. Society is so far off its moral base it can no longer recognize the sin that it is wallowing in.

Proverbs 16:18
James 4:6

Since Adam and Eve's disobedience was the first sin, it is often called the *original sin*. Theologians are right when they tell us that pride is the original sin; it was pride that caused Adam and Eve to think they had what it would take to run their own lives without God.

Ezekiel 18:20
Romans 6:23

One of the great, fixed laws of the universe tells us that sin always brings death. It is a law that makes perfect sense. When a creature sins and becomes worthless to God, there is no good reason to expect him to keep it around cluttering up the universe. Like a burned out light bulb or a dead battery, a sinner is good for nothing but the garbage heap. The black hole of death is the garbage heap of the universe. Death is the means by which God keeps the universe pure.

Ecclesiastes 12:7
Matthew 10:28

The Bible tells us that humans can experience two kinds of death: The first is death of the body; the second is death of the spirit. Death of the body occurs when a person's spirit leaves his or her body. At that point the body ceases to function and begins to decompose.

Luke 16:22-25
Luke 12:4,5

The spirit, however, does not decay into oblivion or cease to exist at death. It remains alive after it leaves the body and exists in a mode of being invisible and incomprehensible to us in a dimension we often call the spiritual world. The human spirit has the capacity to live forever, and God has plans for it to live eternally in unimaginable joy and happiness. He main-

Luke 16:22

tains an army of protective angels that stand ready to escort each human spirit into his presence at the moment they leave the body when the body dies. There they will be refitted with

2 Corinthians 5:1-5

an indestructible body of incredible beauty and perfection (More about this in chapter 12).

However, God's protective angels will respect the wishes of a dying human who has lived his life wanting nothing to do with God. God will not claim a human spirit at death which has declared its independence from him in life; he will allow it to retain the independence it has demanded. It is on its own when it leaves its body, just as it was while it was united with its

56

Revelation 21:8
Matthew 8:12
Matthew 13:41,42
Matthew 25:46
Jude 13
Luke 16:23,24
Mark 9:47,48
Daniel 12:2

Matthew 10:28
2 Thessalonians 1:9

James 1:13-15
Galatians 6:7,8

body. Satan's demonic minions will join with these independent but defenseless spirits in a horrible hell of misery and pain, where they will be separated from God eternally. This tragic end of the independent spirit is known as spiritual death — the ultimate death. Sin brings about both physical and spiritual death.

Whether these outcast spirits will live forever in unrelieved agony or will be annihilated by the forces of hell is a subject of theological debate. Classical Christian theology says that these spirits will experience agony without end in the hideous, unbearable presence of Satan. Although they will be aware and capable of feeling excruciating pain, they will be counted as dead because in the black hole of hell, the trash can of the universe, they will be forever separated from God. Other theologians doubt that these discarded spirits remain alive, but believe that they are annihilated into oblivion. There are two keys to their thinking. The first has to do with the application of the word *eternal*, which they claim does not necessarily mean that torment lasts forever, but that the results of being thrown into hell last forever — the destruction is final and eternally irrevocable. The second is in their understanding of the nature of God's justice. They do not think he would allow any creature to suffer torture forever as payment for only 70 years of sin. The punishment seems out of scale with the crime. Verses that refer to eternal punishment, such as Matthew 25:46, can mean permanent annihilation.

However, it is hardly safe to depend on this interpretation as a means of underestimating the consequences of sin. The first interpretation is not out of the question at all. But what right-thinking person would choose annihilation over eternal ecstasy just to claim the right to live this short life on earth on one's own terms?

Sometimes people wonder why a God who claims to be good would sentence any creature to hell. But we can't blame God because he doesn't send them; they go by their own choice. Everyone is free to choose either God or sin, but according to the natural law, when one chooses sin he also chooses death and must be thrown out into the garbage to keep

Deuteronomy 32:4

the universe clean. God understands that man, with his fallen nature, cannot help but sin. The only way to eliminate sin from creation is to kill the sinner. God does not consign man to death out of spite or cruelty, but of necessity because he is perfect. The simple truth is that sin cannot survive in the same universe with a perfect God. One of them must go, and you can guess which. God could not be called good if he were content to allow evil to have its way forever. Because he is good, he must destroy sin in his universe as a conscientious homeowner exterminates roaches in his house.

If you think goodness is always sweet and gentle, think again. True, unrelenting goodness is a terrifying thing to a sinner, just as true, unrelenting justice is a terrifying thing to a murderer. Much of what people think is God's punishment is really their own evil running on the wrong side of the road and crashing headlong into his goodness. When their lives are shattered in the collision, they unfairly blame God.

Genesis 3:8-19

The Sentence and the Promise

After Adam and Eve sinned, they became so afraid of God's goodness that they tried to hide from him. But, course, hiding from an omniscient and omnipresent God is futile. He called for the cowering couple to come out and stand before him to receive his judgment.

Satan must have worn a smug grin as he watched this cringing pair tremble while waiting to hear their doom. We can imagine him going insane with glee the moment they plainly showed their fallen condition by selfishly passing around the blame for their sin. But he must have been outraged by the unexpected turn that God's judgment took. Adam and Eve had sinned, and Satan knew they deserved to die. He may have expected to see a bolt of lightning explode from heaven and consume them right there on the spot. But instead, God began speaking to the couple about their future and their descendants. What was going on here? They were not supposed to have any future or any descendants. They had violated the universal law; they were supposed to be dead!

Satan is so consumed by hate that he cannot understand

1 John 4:8
1 Peter 1:20,21

Genesis 3:15

Genesis 3:19

love, and this obsession caused him to overlook something about God. God loved this poor couple he had created. Even before he made the world, he had a backup plan already drawn up to take care of the possibility that they would sin. This plan was not an attempt to get around the law of sin and death; God had no intention of breaking universal laws or looking for loopholes in them. The backup plan called for a substitute to stand in the place of the couple and meet the requirements of the law for them. As Adam and Eve stood before God, he made a solemn promise to them that one of their descendants would voluntarily take their death sentence upon himself, die in their place, and crush Satan in the process. Although a few thousand years would pass before this descendant arrived, God knew the plan would work, so he counted it as a sure thing and let Adam and Eve go free.

They were free. They did not have to die on that day, but they had botched things badly. God's promised plan would eventually make things right again between God and themselves, but it could not fix up the mess their sin was to make of their lives on earth. They had played with fire and escaped with their lives, but they would have to live among the ashes and charred framework of their once-perfect world. Now they would have to cope with rebellious appetites and their own unruly human nature. Now they would have to contend with Satan, as their sin had unleashed his evil power and given him a foothold in the world. God's plan would give them a way to save their spirits from the second kind of death — spiritual death — but they could not avoid physical death. Their bodies would wear down and eventually die.

Satan Takes Over

Genesis 3:17-19
Luke 4:5,6
John 14:30
Romans 8:20-22
Ephesians 6:12
1 John 5:19

Satan did not win the total victory he had hoped for in Eden, but he had won an important battle and inflicted enough damage that he apparently thought he might yet win the war. He saw that Adam and Eve were easy targets, and he knew they could no longer give him much resistance, so he moved in. He claimed the earth as conquered territory and set himself up as ruler instead of Adam. With his dreadful army of invisible demons, Satan enslaved nature and turned it against the fallen couple. Weeds, worms, rust, and rot invaded the earth. Poisonous thorns choked delicate flowers; clinging parasites sucked the life from trees, and creeping fungus clogged once-clear streams. Eden was lost. Adam's new home was one of rocks, weeds, and miserly soil. In sweat and tears he and Eve struggled against uncooperative nature for food and shelter.

Satan was right about one thing: Just as he had promised Eve, the unhappy couple learned the difference between good and evil. But they learned it the hard way. Before Adam and Eve lost Eden, they did not think of perfection and joy as anything special or unusual. Goodness was just the ordinary nature of things. People with good teeth tend to take them for granted. It's the poor sufferers with cavities and toothaches who realize how wonderful good teeth are. It never occurred to the unfallen Adam and Eve that all they had was good, because there was nothing bad with which to compare it. They didn't know good because they didn't know evil. Good was simply normal and evil was just a meaningless word. But now, thanks to Satan, they understood the meaning of that word and many others they wished they had never heard — words like pain, grief, fear, weariness, sickness, and death. They expanded their vocabulary, but at a frightful cost. Now they knew that their lost paradise had been good, but it was too late.

A Race of Sinners

Romans 5:12

After Adam and Eve were ejected from Eden, they began to have children. It is important to notice that all of these children would be born in the likeness of their *fallen* parents. Adam and Eve were sinners, and all their descendants would become sinners.

Ezekiel 18:20

There has been some confusion among Christians about this natural fact. Some have thought that because babies are born as fallen creatures like their parents, they are born already guilty of sin. Not so. God is fair and just, and he does not blame where there is no fault. Newborn babies are not guilty of sin, but they are certain to sin in time. A tiger cub will not kill for its food until months after it is born, but we call it a carnivore from birth because it is born into a carnivorous species. Tigers are certain to kill; we are certain to sin.

Isaiah 53:6 Since through Adam and Eve sin was passed on to the entire human race, God's rescue plan was designed to be all inclusive — not just for Adam and Eve alone, but for all their descendants as well. How one person could qualify to take on the penalty for the entire race is the subject of a later chapter.

Questions for Discussion: Chapter 5

1. What is sin?

2. What is meant by the term *original sin*?

3. What are the two kinds of death? Explain both.

4. Why is sin so repugnant to God?

5. Who is now the lord of the earth?

6. How do you see mankind's fallen nature reflected in society today?

7. As a result of the fall, are human children born sinners? Are they born guilty of sin?

6 The People and the Law

After the account of the Fall of Man, the Bible takes up a history of God's dealings with a line of people in ancient times. This record is contained in the first seventeen books of the Old Testament. The Old Testament is so named because it gives us a record of God's first written agreement and promises to mankind. To many Christians, the Old Testament is little more than a confusing jumble of genealogies and stories. Some of the stories are quite familiar, such as those about Noah and the Flood, Moses and the parting of the Red Sea, Joshua and the Battle of Jericho, Samson and Delilah, David and Goliath, and Daniel in the lions' den. But it is important for us to understand the meaning behind these stories, the underlying theme that ties them together, and why they are in the Bible at all.

Of course, the Old Testament accounts are good examples of how God works in the lives of men and women, but they mean much more than that. When you back off and look at the collection of books as a whole, you can see that it tells one, continuous story. That story, in a nutshell, is of God choosing special people and guiding them toward a single, special purpose. That purpose was to prepare a race of people to bring to the world the one who would break the choking grip of Satan from the throat of humanity, as God had promised to Adam and Eve. The entire Old Testament is the account of God at work developing his plan to keep that promise. In this chapter we will look behind the colorful scenes of the Old Testament stories and follow the plan as it unfolds.

The Beginnings

Genesis 5:3-32

For several generations after Adam and Eve lost Eden, men and women had life spans that were incredibly long by today's standards. It was not unusual for a person to live seven or eight centuries, or even more. It may be that the first descendants of humanity's prototype couple retained more of their parents' physical perfection than those who came later, and they simply did not wear down as fast. Or, it may be that Satan's grip on the environment increased with time. Or, it may be, as some suggest, that until the great flood, the earth was shielded by a translucent cloud canopy that shut out the types of sunrays most harmful to the human body.

Adam himself lived to be 930 years old before finally succumbing to death. He and his wife Eve had many children who grew up and had families of their own. But as the population increased, so did Satan's influence; and left unchecked, he might have succeeded in subverting the race completely. But ever since the Fall, there have been a series of strategically placed potholes along the road of history. The purpose of these holes is to jar Satan loose just when he seems on the verge of victory. When evil seems about to dominate, the wheel of progress hits one of these holes. A ruinous disaster shakes up the order of things and checks the spread of evil. This enables man to come to his senses, regroup, get a fresh grip on his principles, and make a new beginning. This bumpy ride of world history has carried the race from Adam to the present, and will continue until the world ends.

Genesis 6-9

Within a few generations after Adam, the human race became more and more evil until finally only one good family was left on the earth. It was time for the first major pothole to jar things up. The only way for God to prevent the worldwide domination of evil was to destroy the race and start over. So he washed the earth clean with a massive flood that drowned everyone alive except that one, good family. Noah, his wife, his three sons, and their wives survived the Flood in a barge-like ship history knows as the ark, along with at least one pair of each species of animal.

Genesis 11:1-8

Satan was undaunted by the Flood. Before the ark was dry, he launched a new campaign against Noah's descendants. As man repopulated the earth, each new generation grew more powerful and sophisticated than the last. And Satan saw to it that each new generation also grew more proud and arrogant. In time, men again rejected God and enthroned themselves in his place, just as Adam and Eve had done. At the peak of their folly, they began to construct a towering skyscraper from which they intended to rule the world according to their own man-centered philosophies.

Then came another pothole. God put an effective stop to this rebellion without resorting to catastrophe. Up to this point in history, everyone on the earth spoke the same language. But at a given moment while the tower was well under construction, God touched man's tongue and divided his speech into diverse languages. Suddenly, chaos disrupted construction. The workers could not communicate, because the simplest request or command sounded to the hearer like a tape player running in reverse. When a bricklayer asked for a drink, his assistant might fetch him a tar bucket. The tower project ended in confusion, and people scattered throughout the earth, grouping with those who shared their new languages. The unfinished skyscraper was called the tower of Babel. Babel ("babble") means confusion.

When the people scattered from Babel, new cities sprang up across the earth. Some of these cities prospered and became great civilizations that were rich and powerful. But in their prosperity, they forgot the lesson of Adam, the Flood, and the Tower of Babel. Again they let Satan turn them away from God, and they began to worship stars, images, animals, and spirits.

Genesis 11:26-31   One of the richest and most powerful of these cities was Ur, in the land of the Chaldees (the present country of Iran). In that city lived a man named Abram (later renamed Abraham). Young Abraham managed to remain true to God in spite of all the rampant evil around him. On finding such a strong faith in such a pagan world, God chose Abraham as the key person to set in motion the series of events that would ultimately fulfill his promise to Adam.

Genesis 12:1-3   God instructed Abraham to leave his father's household and
Genesis 22:17,18   sent him off toward a distant, unknown land. As Abraham prepared for the journey, God made a solemn promise to him.

65

He promised that Abraham's descendants would become a great nation with a population as uncountable as the stars in the nighttime sky or the grains of sand on the seashore. And from these descendants would rise the promised chosen One who would come armed with the power to break the death grip of Satan forever.

To prepare for the coming of this pivotal event in human history, God began to form that special nation from Abraham's children. He chose Abraham's grandson Jacob to become its founding father. Young Jacob hardly fit the mold of a national patriarch; he was a conniver and a cheat in his early days. But in his mature years he earned the name Israel, which means, "One who struggles with God." His new name confirmed that through his struggles he had won a new nature from God. Jacob had twelve sons who became fathers of twelve thriving tribes. These tribes later became individual provinces when the nation of Israel was founded.

Of all Jacob's sons, Joseph was his obvious favorite. The other sons became jealous of the gifts and attention their father lavished on the boy. The brothers' jealousy swelled into hate, and they sold Joseph to a caravan of slave traders headed for Egypt. But in Egypt Joseph rose from slavery to become the nation's prime minister and devised a plan that saved the land from severe famine. Years later Joseph was reconciled to his brothers. He arranged to bring their families into Egypt to avoid starvation brought on by the drought that was also ravaging their homeland.

After Jacob and Joseph died, a new pharaoh came to the Egyptian throne who felt no obligation to the memory of Joseph. He ruthlessly enslaved the growing Israeli population and put them under the lash building his memorial cities. The captive nation endured in Egypt for over 400 years while they grew to a population of perhaps two or three million hardy people.

When the slavery became unbearable, God raised up from among the Israelis the dedicated leader Moses, whose name still stands as one of the great men in human history. God used the hand of Moses to topple the power of Egypt with a series

Genesis 27:36
Genesis 32:28

Genesis 49

Genesis 37–50

Exodus 1–15

of spectacular and devastating plagues. When the crushed Egyptians could endure no more, Moses led Israel out of Egypt through the miraculously parted Red Sea and on toward a land of their own.

The Law

Exodus 19

On the way to the promised land, God halted the Israeli nation and had them camp at the foot of the mysterious, thundering Mount Sinai. God called Moses up to the fiery summit of that mountain and gave him a set of laws to govern the

Exodus 20

people's behavior and worship. These laws included the Ten Commandments and a long slate of subsidiary rules that went into considerable detail on the maintenance of relationships, health, property, farmland, government, and worship. All these laws taken together are generally known as "the Law."

The Law plays such a significant role in the history of man's relationship to God that it is worthwhile to pause in our march through the Old Testament to explain why it was given and how it works. In reality, there was nothing new about the Law as God gave it to Moses on Sinai. It was not an outline of some new kind of morality or guidelines to an innovative or different mode of human behavior. The ideal code of behavior for humans known as the Moral Law had never been a secret to mankind, even before Sinai. The ancient Babylonian monarch Hammurabi, who predated Moses by about 300 years, codified a set of moral laws almost identical to the Ten Commandments.

Romans 2:14,15

All mankind from Adam to now has intuitively known these

Psalm 40:8

basic rules that ought to govern all human relationships; but at Sinai God made these rules official. He gave them legal force by putting them in writing, leaving his people no excuse for ignorance of his will.

Many people, believers and nonbelievers alike, have a common misunderstanding of the purpose of the Law. They tend to see it as a list of restrictive "don'ts" that throws cold water on the best kinds of fun and places limits on enjoyment. Actually, the opposite is true. The Law shows us how to channel our desires to bring about the greatest possible fulfillment of

Psalm 37:4

them. All desires are God-given and meant to be fulfilled and enjoyed. All of them. Our problem as fallen humans is not that we have illegitimate desires, but that we look for illegitimate ways to satisfy them. We get impatient with the winding road to fulfillment and take off on a shortcut through the underbrush. But the shortcut doesn't get us where we want to go. The illegitimate satisfaction of desire turns out to be empty, and the shortcut infested with predators and pitted with quicksand.

To illustrate how the Law protects us from these perils, let's take a look at one of its universally recognized tenets — the institution of marriage. Every society since the beginning of history has required that the privileges of love between man and woman be sanctioned by marriage. God ordained the law of marriage to insure the commitment of mates to each other and to the children they produce. Fallen humans need such a law because the strength of sexual desire often overcomes the will and leads them to take a shortcut around marriage, bypassing the responsibility in order to get straight to the pleasure. But when the bloom is plucked, it dies. Pleasure separated from the responsibilities of commitment and creation withers into meaninglessness. And to make matters worse, the shortcut leads through a tangled mass of guilts, fears, betrayals, broken relationships, diseases, unwanted children, and other complications.

The Law gives us marriage as the means by which we can satisfy the desire for a mate without encountering these complications. Of course, marriage may seem insipid, restrictive, confining, and boring to those who knuckle under to the demands of unrestrained desire. They cannot imagine how sticking to one partner year in and year out can possibly be fulfilling. But those who strap themselves into the marriage relationship and ride out its ups and downs will find continuing and growing fulfillment because the deeper desire within sexual desire is the longing for oneness. The bed hopper who thinks the object of sex is physical gratification mocks the ideal of oneness with his multiple encounters. He will grow increasingly frustrated in his quest for fulfillment. Each brief encounter is meaningless because it does not touch the deeper joys of committed relationship. Those who stick by their vows and

James 1:14,15

Genesis 2:24
Mark 10:9
Hebrews 13:4
Proverbs 6:23-34

Proverbs 5:15-19

truly love will fly into realms of joy the the uncommitted cannot possibly imagine.

1 Timothy 1:9,10 We need the Law because we would not of our own volition choose the harder, higher road. Commitment does not come easy for us; the fallen self resists compromising its own freedom. The temptation is always there to avoid the hard decision and take the shortcut to immediate pleasure. The vows of marriage are a promise between partners that they will not yield to the pull of self, but will stay on the road prescribed by Law.

The law of marriage is only one example of the Moral Law, but it illustrates the Law's purpose. Law maps out the path to fulfillment and warns of deceptive shortcuts that may look more direct and promising. It is an owner's manual that tells us how to run and maintain the human machine. It shows us how to avoid unhappiness and how to achieve the greatest satisfaction to our God-given desires. That, in a nutshell, is the Law.

Soon after receiving the Law on Mount Sinai, the people of Israel found that in spite of their best efforts, they obeyed it very poorly. However, God was not at all surprised. He knew before he gave the Law that the people would not obey it. Only perfect people obey the Law perfectly — people like Adam and Eve before they fell into sin. In fact, the Law was essentially a description of how a perfect, unfallen person would behave. But the nation of Israel was not made up of perfect, unfallen people; they were sinners like Adam and Eve after the Fall.

If obedience to the Law was impossible, why did God give it? Why saddle his people with a standard that he knew was beyond their abilities? God gave Israel the Law so they could see the truth about themselves. He understood humanity's fallen condition very clearly, but he wanted them to understand Romans 3:20 it as well. He gave them the Law so they could see that they were sin-damaged creatures incapable of living their lives in harmony with his perfect universe. The Law was a yardstick that showed how people must live in order to be what they were created to be. They could compare their real behavior to the standard of the Law and see that they did not measure up.

Romans 7:18

The Law showed them plainly that it is absolutely impossible for a fallen creature to be good. It showed them that the human race needed God back in their lives in order to function according to the universal moral standard.

Hebrews 9–10

Hebrews 9:22

There was another side to the Law that had nothing to do with personal morality. The edicts from Sinai included instructions for instituting and conducting various ceremonies and feasts. These ceremonies were symbols that hinted at the shape of God's plan to pay the death-price for man's sin. Many of them required the people of Israel to sacrifice to God some of the finest animals from their flocks and herds. These sacrifices were meant to help the people show that they recognized their fallen condition and needed God's forgiveness for their failure to keep the Law. Of course, killing animals could not even come close to paying the price for sin, but the ritual shedding of blood established the concept that nothing short of death would be required to pay for it. In addition, these sacrifices encouraged the people to give willingly of their finest possessions to God, because he was planning to do no less for them.

Although the Law was too pure for the fallen people of Israel to obey, the mere attempt at obedience improved their lives enough to make it worth the effort. Blinking and squinting in the glare of pure light is a big improvement over bumping around in the dark. Even Israel's stumbling attempts to follow the Law made them healthier, happier, more prosperous, and nearer to God than they could have been without it.

Questions for Discussion: Chapter 6

1. What is the purpose of the Old Testament?

2. Why is the repeated cycle of history one of beginnings, progress, disaster and new beginnings?

3. Why was it wrong to build the Tower of Babel?

4. Were the tables of stone given to Moses on Mt. Sinai man's first exposure to the Moral Law?

5. What is the purpose of the Law?

6. Could the people of Israel obey the Law? Was God surprised at this?

7. Why did God give the Law if he knew the people couldn't obey it?

7 The Chosen People

Numbers 10:11-13   Armed with the Law and with hearts full of hope, the
people of Israel struck their tents, left Mount Sinai, and began
their march toward the promised land of Canaan, which lay at
Joshua 3:10   the eastern end of the Mediterranean Sea. At this time Canaan
was occupied by a number of corrupt and depraved tribes —
all those multi-pronounceable "ites" — the Canaanites,
Hittites, Hivites, Perizzites, Girgashites, Amorites, Jebusites
and, of course, the Philistines. God's plan was to fell two trees
with one stroke. He intended to have the army of Israel exter-
minate these abominable tribes, and in the process, earn their
own homeland.

Numbers 13,14   But on the very borders of Canaan, the people balked. Ten
of the twelve spies Moses sent into the land returned to the
camp with alarming reports: Canaan was filled with enormous
warrior giants and impregnable walled fortresses. The people
were stunned. Since God had promised them the land, they
expected just to march in and take it with little effort. They
wanted their gift assembled, set up, and ready to use. These
newly-freed people of Israel had spent their entire lives as
dependent slaves under Egyptian masters. They lacked the
courage and initiative needed to take Canaan by force from
such formidable opposition.

God was ready to give the people certain victory had they
merely trusted him. He was highly displeased with their faint-
hearted lack of faith. Although they stood on the very threshold
Numbers 14:30-35   of their promised homeland, God turned them back and
sentenced them to wander in the bleak desert of Sinai and
Midian for forty years. Those who had been slaves in Egypt died
in this wasteland while a new generation — bolder, hardier,
more courageous, and more faithful — grew to adulthood.

At the end of the forty years, God brought the new generation of Israelis to the border of Canaan. Just as the people were
Deuteronomy 34:1-8 finally ready to cross the Jordan River into their promised land,
Moses climbed to the top of Mount Nebo and God took him.
Joshua 1:1-9 His second-in-command, a tough, upright, unbending general
named Joshua took over and led Israel into their long-awaited
home.
Joshua 2–24 City by city Joshua conquered most of the inhabitants of the
territory, and the people began to set up housekeeping in their
new homeland.
Judges 2:16– At first the new nation of Israel experienced a period of
1 Samuel 8 disorder and lawlessness. Society disintegrated as the people
drifted away from the Law and began to live by doing their
own thing. The historical accounts of human depravity in the
book of Judges are among the most appalling in the Bible. The
Judges 21:25 book tells us that, "In those days Israel had no king; everyone
did as he saw fit." When the anarchy became so pervasive that
an entire tribe was almost annihilated, the nation began to be
ruled somewhat loosely by a succession of God-appointed
leaders called judges.* The list of judges contains several well-
Judges 7 known names such as Gideon, who defeated a massive army of
Judges 11 Midianite invaders with only 300 men; and Jephthah, the
warrior-judge whose rash vow cost him his only daughter.
Possibly the best-known and most colorful of the judges was
Judges 13–16 Samson, strong of body but weak of will. Samson was a man
of supernatural strength who wrought havoc on Israel's
Philistine oppressors. Samson's Philistine mistress Delilah
cajoled him into revealing that the secret of his strength was in
a vow that he would never cut his hair. She lulled him to sleep
and had him shorn. With his strength gone, he was blinded and
imprisoned. When the Philistines brought Samson to the
temple of their god Dagon to celebrate their victory over him,
he prayed to God for a final surge of strength. The prayer was
granted. He broke the key pillars of the temple, causing it to
collapse and kill 3,000 Philistine celebrants as well as himself.
1 Samuel 8– As the nation grew, the people began to want a king. They
1 Kings 12

*The book of Judges is not altogether sequential. The events in chapters 17 through 21
occur prior to those in chapters 1 through 16. (See Numbers 25:7-11; Judges 20:27,28.)

felt a king would unify the country and enforce the law, but mostly they wanted a king because all the nations around them had kings. Therefore, the last judge Samuel reluctantly anointed a king over Israel and ushered in the beginning of the nation's golden age. During the next 120 years, the little nation grew to become the richest and most powerful kingdom in that part of the world.

1 Samuel 9–31

Three successive kings led Israel through this period. The first was Saul. Saul was an impressive looking man — a head taller than anyone else in Israel — whose reign began with great promise but ended in personal ruin as he was gripped by severe depression and raging jealousy.

The object of Saul's jealousy was a young shepherd named David. Handsome, brilliant, brave, and musically talented, David's star rose as Saul's was falling. David had become a national hero in his teen years when he felled the seemingly

1 Samuel 17

invincible giant Philistine warrior Goliath. He went on to become a successful general and an inspiring poet, winning the

2 Samuel 1,2
2 Samuel 2–24

hearts of the people both with valor and song. When Saul died in battle, David became king, and during his 40-year reign built the nation into a power to be reckoned with.

1 Kings 1–11

David's son Solomon followed his father to the throne. Solomon was renowned for his great wisdom, and finally for his great folly. He added extravagance and opulence to the

1 Kings 4:20-28

growing empire he inherited. Partly to form alliances, and partly because of his own tendency toward excess, Solomon

1 Kings 11:3
1 Kings 5–6

married 700 wives and took on 300 additional concubines. He built a magnificent temple in the capital city of Jerusalem where his people could assemble to worship God. But at the

1 Kings 11:1-8

same time, to appease wives and politicians, he allowed false religions from neighboring countries to set up places of worship in Israel. The attractive but immoral sexual pleasures these false gods offered began to lure men away from the stabilizing influence of the Law. Another pothole in the road of history was about to shake things up.

Division and Captivity

1 Kings 12:1-19

In time the people began to resent the heavy burden of taxes imposed on them to maintain the excesses of the king's court. When King Solomon died, his son Rehoboam took the throne and threatened to increase the taxes levied by his father. It was more than the people could take; unrest in the nation boiled over and the country split in two. The northern ten tribes divided from the southern tribes of Judah and Benjamin. The north retained the name Israel while the south took the name of its dominant tribe Judah.

After the split, northern Israel began to self-destruct. Cut off from the temple in Jerusalem (located in Judah), the people abruptly turned from God to the sensual false religions of their neighbors. All the northern kings were corrupt. Many of them succeeded to the throne by murdering their predecessors. In spite of warnings from prophets such as Elijah and Elisha, these people ignored the Law and soon became slaves to their own unbridled desires and senses. Finally, God gave up on the northern tribes and allowed the Assyrians to conquer and deport them. The Israelis were scattered among foreign nations where they gradually mixed and blended into oblivion. Thus northern Israel vanished and never existed again.

For over two hundred years after the division, the southern nation of Judah managed to avoid the rapid slide downward that had doomed the north. One reason for their relative stability was that the ruling dynasty remained intact. The line of kings remained in the family of David. Another reason was that they had a focal point for the worship of God in their temple at Jerusalem. But it was not enough. The idol worship brought in by Solomon was a corrupting poison that slowly spread throughout the weakened nation. They began to slip out of the hand of God to gratify the demands of self. The downward slide was slowed once or twice by reform-minded kings such as Hezekiah and Josiah who tried to lead the nation to repentance, but the fatal descending spiral had gained too much momentum. It could not be reversed.

Toward the end, God sent prophets such as Isaiah and Jeremiah to urge Judah to turn back to the Law, but the people would not listen. Finally, God had to step in and stop the cycle of sin with another act of destruction. He allowed

1 Kings 12:25-33

1 Kings 12–
2 Kings 17

2 Kings 17:1-40

2 Kings 18–25

2 Kings 18,22,23

2 Kings 25
2 Chronicles 36:15-
20

the Babylonians to conquer the nation of Judah and deport its citizens to Babylon.

Judah's reaction to calamity was altogether different from that of Israel. They resisted the chameleon-like blending into their captors' wallpaper that had caused their northern brothers to vanish. The trauma of captivity shocked many of the people of Judah (called Jews) into remembering the Law. Homesick and penitent, they dusted off the old scrolls and made a serious effort to learn the Law and follow its directives.

These exiled Jews, living as second-class citizens in the country of their conquerors, were often despised and mistreated. For example, they were denied the right to work at most of the favored occupations. As a result, many of them became merchants and money lenders, giving rise to an unfair but persistent ethnic stereotype that still endures. These Jews huddled together in isolated communities and turned for comfort to their study, their worship, their families, and their traditions. They longed for the golden days of the past when their nation was independent and respected. They savored the stories of their national heroes and began to take seriously the promises of deliverance from captivity they found in the writings of their prophets.

Many of these prophecies foretold the coming of the promised One, called the Messiah, who would deliver mankind from the death-grip of sin. But for the most part, these Jews were blinded to this greater truth by their immediate need. They interpreted the promise to mean deliverance and reestablishment of their own nation and nothing more. They expected their Messiah to be a military and political leader who would lead them to freedom and national glory. They did not understand that the feast God was preparing was meant to feed the entire world; they thought it was meant only to fill their own empty plates.

The 1971 movie *Fiddler on the Roof* showed vividly how displaced Jews carried on with their unique lives in the midst of hostile environments. Although this movie was about Jews who lived in Russia in the early 1900's — twenty-four centuries after the captivity of Judah — it gave a clear picture of how

Jews in general have been poorly treated in foreign lands. It showed them banding together and tenaciously keeping their law and traditions intact in spite of revolution and change threatening from all sides. The lives of the deported Jews in Babylon must have been very similar.

Daniel 1:18-20

Daniel 6:1-3

Daniel 6

But not all Jews remained confined to the ghettos of Babylon. A number of them rose to hold high positions in the governments of their captors. The deported Jew Daniel became chief counselor and high official of the Babylonian and Persian kings. His unflinching devotion to God caused his jealous political rivals to have him thrown into a den of starving lions. But when God miraculously kept him from harm, even the king became a believer.

Ezra 1:1-3

Esther 1–10

Fifty years after Babylon conquered Judah, Cyrus the Persian conquered Babylon. When a later king, Xerxes, became the Persian emperor, he chose a stunningly beautiful Jewish girl named Esther to be his queen. Esther was as brave as she was beautiful. The story of how she risked her life to save her people from annihilation at the hand of an evil, conspiring palace official is one of the most dramatic and thrilling in the Bible. Esther's cousin Mordecai rose by his unwavering integrity from doorkeeper of the king's palace to prime minister of the Persian empire.

Nehemiah 1:11–2:9

A godly Jew named Nehemiah was a personal servant to the Persian emperor Artaxerxes. Having access to the ear of the king, Nehemiah told him of the Jews' longing to return to their homeland. Artaxerxes not only signed the decree authorizing the return, he provided funds and assistance for the rebuilding of their cities. The Jewish priest Ezra had the backing of Artaxerxes, including funds and assistance for rebuilding the destroyed temple in Jerusalem as well.

Ezra 7:12-25

Return to the Homeland

Ezra, Nehemiah

Ezra 1:1-11

Old Testament history ends as the exiled Jews return to their country. The Persian emperors Cyrus, Artaxerxes, and Darius all allowed groups of captives to return. Cyrus actually instigated the rebuilding of the temple. Under the leadership of men like Ezra and Nehemiah, the Jews began to rebuild their cities, their temple, their nation, and their singular way of life. They rebuilt and resettled, but the days of strength and glory were gone. The little nation of Judah was pushed and shoved by every power that crisscrossed their land in the endless wars and invasions that have always plagued that part of the world.

In the gap of time between the Old and New Testaments (about 400 years), the Jews were conquered again as the Greeks swept through the Mediterranean nations in their quest for world dominion. But Judah became independent again when a family of brothers known as the Maccabees (which means "the Hammerers") led a successful revolt. The Jews then governed themselves for about 100 years. But their independence ended abruptly when the irresistible force of the Roman Empire invaded and set up a puppet government under Caesar.

In spite of these endless wars and invasions, the determined Jews went on with their ancestral record keeping. At the beginning of the New Testament, we find the records of one family of particular importance. This family had kept the records of its lineage intact in an unbroken line all the way from Adam. Their lineage continued through Abraham, Judah, David, Solomon, and finally, after many centuries, it led to an insignificant carpenter named Joseph who lived in the insignificant little Jewish village of Nazareth. Joseph was the last link in the chain of people God chose to bring into the world the Messiah. Now everything was ready; the time was right, the stage was set, the lights were up, and the curtain was ready to be drawn.

Matthew 1:1-17

Questions for Discussion: Chapter 7

1. Why was it just for God to have the people of Israel win their homeland by slaughtering the tribes that lived there?

2. Do you see any parallels between Israel and our nation today in the following?
   A. The period of the Judges
   B. Solomon's bringing idol worship to the nation for political reasons.

3. Is there any connection between moral degeneration and political decline? Explain.

4. Why did the nation of Israel divide? Why did Judah outlast northern Israel?

5. Can a nation's momentum toward destruction be reversed?

6. How did Judah's reaction to captivity differ from northern Israel's? Why this difference?

7. What did the Jews expect from the coming Messiah?

8 God Comes to Earth

Matthew 1:18-25 Joseph, a carpenter of Nazareth, a village in the Roman occupied province of Judah (called Judea in the New Testament) was a direct descendant of the great king David. He was a solid, upright, God-believing, law-abiding Jewish citizen engaged to marry a Jewish girl named Mary, who was also a descendant of David.

To Joseph's shock and dismay, he found that Mary was pregnant. He knew the baby was not his, so naturally he decided not to marry the girl. He quietly made plans to break the engagement. However, an angel came to him in a dream and convinced him that Mary was indeed an innocent virgin in spite of the fact that she was pregnant. Furthermore, the angel told Joseph that the baby to be born to Mary was God's own Son. This was an astounding announcement, but Joseph believed it. He believed already in a supernatural God, so he did not find it incredible that such a God could cause this supernatural event. Without further hesitation he went on with the wedding.

Luke 2:1-7 When it came time for the baby to be born, Mary and Joseph had traveled from Nazareth to the home of their ancestral roots in Bethlehem to comply with the procedures of the Roman census. All tourist accommodations were full, so they took a stable for shelter. And there the baby was born. The promise to Adam and Eve, to Abraham, to Jacob, Judah, and David was delivered in a shelter for animals. The one hope of lifting the human race out of the quagmire of sin lay in a feeding trough. The only power in the universe capable of crushing the head of Satan lay as a baby under the watchful eyes of Joseph and Mary. They named him Jesus, which means *savior.*

The God Who Came Down from Heaven

It is important that we understand a few things about the nature and background of Jesus, because he could not have done what he did had he not been who he was. There were certain requirements to be met and certain powers to be exercised that demanded a being exactly like Jesus to make the promised plan work.

Philippians 2:5-8

John 1:1-4,14

What made the baby in the feeding trough unique was that before he was born that day in Bethlehem, he had been God in heaven. He had enjoyed full equality with God the Father and God the Holy Spirit. When he allowed himself to be placed in a baby's body to be inserted into the human race as a man, he willingly surrendered his divine position and presumably his power (the Bible does not define exactly what "emptied himself" means). However, he did not cease to be God. Jesus was exactly the same being after his birth into our race as he had been before. Some of his relationships and responsibilities changed, but not his essence. We are correct in thinking that Jesus was still God after his birth in Bethlehem; he was still the same omnipotent being who had created the universe. But in another sense, you could say that he was no longer God because he gave up his throne — his position or "job" as God in heaven — to live and act strictly as a man in a fully human body.

Philippians 2:7

(RSV/NASB)

Let's try to clarify this concept with a parable. The president of a large corporation went to the chairman of the board and said, "We are having a continuing problem, and the only way to correct it is to take drastic and unorthodox measures. Our janitorial staff is not keeping our building clean, and a dirty building is a bad reflection on our company. I have sent them detailed instructions to follow and hired experts to teach them how to do the work, but they're still not getting it right. So I have decided to go down and work with them myself for a while to show them personally how we want the job done. While I am doing this, I would like for you to take over the operation of the company." So the president closed his office, changed from business suit to work clothes, and instructed the employment office to arrange for him a job as janitor. Then he took up his broom and worked side by side with the regular janitors as one of them, and taught them all his janitorial requirements.

While this executive was working with the cleaning crew, he was not performing as the company president. The chairman of the board had taken the president's share of the power and made all the decisions that kept the company going. He even gave orders to the new janitor. Yet the president-turned-janitor was still the same person he had always been; he was the man who knew the company's inner workings and still possessed the talent and skills he had used to guide it to success. Nevertheless, at the moment the company records listed him as a mere janitor, and he took his orders from the chairman just as any good worker should.

John 1:14

Colossians 1:15-17

It was much the same with Jesus. When he came to the earth, he was the same person with the same capabilities and powers he had possessed while in heaven. The man who walked right here on our planet at a specific moment in our history had the strength and know-how to make and unmake worlds, to control natural forces, to be in all places at all moments. But when he was born in Bethlehem, he left all these powers with God the Father, voluntarily accepted all the limitations and responsibilities of humanity, and became a human being cast in the same mold as Adam.

The Perfect Human

In chapter three we defined what it means to be human. A human is a creature designed to be filled with God and directed by him. None of us functions as designed because we are fallen creatures — we kick God out. No one born after Adam fell has ever reflected *true* humanity — that is, humanity which perfectly reflects the nature of God — because all of Adam's descendants bear the effects of the Fall. So when Jesus came, he showed us something we could never see by looking at each other; in him we saw what a human is like when he functions exactly as designed. In Jesus we saw the first example of perfect humanity that had lived on the earth since Adam. When Jesus gave up his right to absolute, universal authority and let

John 5:19-20

Philippians 2:8

83

John 8:29
John 12:49
John 14:10,11

John 6:38

Matthew 4:1-4

God the Father direct his life, he voluntarily reshaped his solid, complete, and all-sufficient spirit into the hollow, cup-shaped spirit of humanity. It was something like melting down a golden crown and recasting it into a goblet. Then God the Father poured his own Holy Spirit into the golden cup of Jesus' spirit. From that point on, Jesus let the Father give all the orders and did nothing except what the Father directed him to do. Jesus was fully God, and nothing less; but on that day in Bethlehem, he laid aside his rights as God and became fully man and nothing more. Although he was God, he lived his life solely as a man, obedient to the will of the Father in heaven exactly as Adam lived before the Fall.

"But," you may ask, "What about the miracles Jesus performed? Don't they show him to be acting as God instead of man?" The answer is no, because Jesus did not perform these miracles by his own power; he merely acted as the agent of the Father's power. He was the transmitter of the signal, not the broadcaster. And we must remember that Jesus was not the first to work miracles. God-directed men such as Moses and Elijah frequently performed supernatural acts, but they, like Jesus, performed them as deputies of God in heaven, not by their own inherent power.

Had Jesus decided to perform miracles by his own power, the implications would have been staggering. At the outset of Jesus' ministry when he was fasting in the desert, Satan tried to get him to satisfy his hunger by turning stones into bread. Jesus refused, and we must be eternally grateful that he did. That simple miracle would have undone his ministry. God the Father had decreed at creation that stones should be stones. For the Son to take one of those stones and say, "No, that is to be bread," would have been a contradiction of the Father's will. To perform such a miracle on his own initiative Jesus would have been forced to step out of his obedient role as man acting as God's agent. He would have to reassert his own rights as one of the Godhead and perform the miracle by his own innate power instead of depending on the power of God the Father working in him. Such an independent act on Jesus' part would have undone Jesus' mission on earth, because by acting as God

Jesus would have lost his status as man, and as we shall soon see, it was necessary for Jesus to be a man in order to qualify to rescue the human race from enslavement by Satan. Indeed, it is reasonable to suppose that if Jesus had contradicted the will of the Father by taking Satan's dare, it would probably have undone the universe itself. How could creation survive with its sustainers at odds with each other? By remaining hungry, Jesus remained a man and held steady on his mission to give humanity a path back to a full relationship with God.

Matthew 4:2,17

After spending forty days fasting in the desert, Jesus began his ministry to mankind. For the next three years, he circulated among the people of Judea, healing, teaching, training, and giving them full exposure to his perfect humanity. At first thought it may seem to us callous and cruel for Jesus to parade his perfection before a damaged race that couldn't possibly live up to his standard. Flaunting his flawless example in the faces of imperfect sinners as if to say, "You should be like me," seems somewhat like having an Olympic sprinter give a demonstration on running to the participants in a wheelchair derby. The sprinter's superior athletic ability would not encourage the handicapped competitors to do better; more likely it would discourage them into giving up. Watching a healthy runner make his laps would do nothing to help the handicapped out of their wheelchairs. The contrast between themselves and the runner would serve only to underscore the hopelessness of their condition. A paraplegic does not need an example; he needs a cure.

The problem with the human race was that they did not know they needed a cure. In a land where absolutely everyone is wheelchair bound, it would be easy to assume that the condition must be normal and dismiss the idea of men walking as an idealistic fantasy in the same category as traveling at the speed of light. The human race had lost sight of the ideal of human perfection. The concept of a perfect human was utterly foreign to their experience, so they dismissed it as an impossible

Romans 3:20

dream. They had the Law to show them the rules for human perfection, but they had corrupted the use of the Law. It was

Galatians 3:24

meant to be used as a medical reference is used — to show

them that they had a disease that needed attention. But instead of using the Law as a diagnostic tool, they tried to take it as a cure. The Jews made the mistake of thinking that learning the Law perfectly would make them perfect, or so close to perfect that God should, in fairness, simply ignore the difference.

Matthew 23:23

But learning the Law could no more make one perfect than learning a medical book could make one well. Even the most thorough knowledge of podiatry or spinal injuries will not enable a wheelchair-bound person to take a single step. We humans needed a cure for the fatal disease of sin that infected the entire race, but we would not seek treatment because we did not know we were sick. Jesus had to show us our need before he could do anything to help us.

In effect, Jesus said to us by his example: "I am a model of true humanity as humanity was meant to be. I am perfect, and you may think this makes me exceptional; but it does not. Perfection is merely normal in the eyes of God. For a man or woman to be anything less is to be subhuman. You are not what God intends a human to be until you become like me." Thus the perfect example of Jesus confronted man with the seriousness of his dilemma. If the minimum requirement that God will accept is absolute perfection, our case is hopeless. None of us measures up.

Matthew 5:48

John 8:52,53
John 9:22,26-34
John 10:33

The Jews had become so proud of their lawkeeping that they hated Jesus and his irksome perfection, and we can understand why: The truth was too hard to take. It meant that humanity's sinful condition hopelessly doomed them to be swept into the dump heap of hell, and there was nothing they could do about it. Hard though it is, this is exactly the truth Jesus intended to show us in his own life. It was necessary for us to understand our condition so we would accept his solution. One who thinks he is healthy will not search for a cure.

The Substitute

Standing squarely between Jesus and the remedy for the human condition was that universal law of sin and death. This law (which we defined in chapter five) should not be confused with the Moral Law ("The Law") that God gave the people of

Romans 6:23

Israel at Sinai. The universal law of sin and death is what placed the race under a heavy curse when Adam fell. It is the law that said *the soul that sins must die.* That law sealed our doom, for we are a race of born sinners. The death of a sinner as demanded by this law is eternal separation from God. There was no way for Jesus to get around that unchangeable law. He had to meet it head on to free us from its doom. The grim, unavoidable fact was that he would have to die himself as a substitute for the fallen human race. Just as in Dickens' *A Tale of Two Cities* Sidney Carton took the place of the husband of the woman he loved and went to the guillotine for him, Jesus came down from heaven to take our place as sinners condemned by the universal law.

For Jesus to qualify as our substitute, he had to have two attributes that could not be naturally combined in a single being: He had to be sinless, and he had to be a member of Adam's race. Adam broke the universal law; the sentence was levied against his race; so his race was obligated to pay the penalty. The solution to the uniquely human problem of sin had to come from within the human family. The price had to be paid by the sacrifice of human life. When Jesus was born that day in Bethlehem, he became one of us — a human; a relative by blood and lineage to our forefather Adam.

Our substitute had to be sinless for obvious reasons. No sinner could qualify as a substitute for other sinners because his life would be forfeit for his own sins. Anyone who sins is himself condemned by the universal law. A substitute would have to be utterly sinless to be free from the curse of the law. A man dying of heart disease cannot be a heart donor to another with the same malady. Only a healthy heart will do.

The need for humanity's substitute to be both human and sinless posed a dilemma that required a divine solution. Adam's race, left to itself, never produced a sinless human. The only being apparently capable of living a perfect, sinless life in a sin-damaged world dominated by Satan was God himself. God would remain unfallen in the face of the evil and temptation that infested the earth, because sin is foreign to his nature. But God was not a human, and the Law required a

Ecclesiastes 7:20

1 Corinthians
15:21,22
Hebrews 2:14

Psalm 14:1-3
Isaiah 53:6
Romans 3:23
Psalm 18:30
Matthew 5:48

human sacrifice. To resolve the dilemma, the second member of the Godhead inserted himself into a human body. He was born into our race as a natural descendant of Adam and lived his life exactly as a perfect human should. Since he had no sins of his own to account for, and since he was now a member of the human family, he qualified fully as our substitute.

Jesus did not come to show us up; he came to solve our dilemma. We were sin-damaged creatures living subhuman lives, doomed to eternal death because we lacked the means of getting free of our sinful condition. The only solution was to find a perfect substitute to die in our place. Jesus came to be that substitute.

Hebrews 2:9

Questions for Discussion: Chapter 8

1. In what sense was Jesus still God while he lived on earth? In what sense was he human?

2. Why didn't Jesus perform miracles on his own initiative?

3. What did Jesus show us by living a perfect human life? Does he expect us to live perfect lives?

4. Can learning the law and living by it make up for sin? Why?

5. Why did Jesus have to be both human and perfect?

6. Since Jesus was God and God cannot sin, could Jesus have sinned? Why or why not?

.

9 The Defeat of Satan

It might seem that the enormous importance of the sacrifice of Jesus would have merited great pomp and fanfare. We might expect that God would have had angelic sentinels in place and celestial trumpets blaring as Jesus marched from the judgment throne to a gilded altar of execution. As he ascended the steps, the majestic tones of a heavenly choir would sing of the heroic God who left heaven to suffer death for his own creation. But the real event was nothing like this.

Those who judged and executed Jesus had no idea of the cosmic significance of their act. The Jews who brought him to trial thought they were getting rid of a heretic whose growing popularity was threatening their powerful religious establishment. The Romans who executed him did so for sheer political reasons. Governor Pontius Pilate, who pronounced the death sentence, knew that Jesus was innocent, but he gave in to the angry Jewish mob to prevent a possible riot or uprising. For Jesus there was no honor, no glory, no sign of gratitude, and virtually no sympathy. The Son of God who came to save the race was ridiculed, beaten, humiliated, and brutally nailed to a crude cross to die as a common criminal. Like a dog that bites the hand that frees it from a trap, our race executed the man who freed us from our sins. And that very execution was the means by which he set us free.

John 11:45-49

John 19:4
John 19:12-16

The Death of Jesus

John 19:17
1 Peter 2:24

John 19:30
Romans 5:15,19

Jesus trudged toward the Place of the Skull where he was crucified — hung by nails driven through his hands and feet to a Roman cross where he endured six hours of agony before he died. At the end of his ordeal, he gave a great shout to heaven declaring, "It is finished!" And it was. The price was paid. One

Hebrews 9:16-28 man brought sin into the world, and one man took the penalty for sin. The law was satisfied; the books were balanced.

John 19:38-42 Followers of Jesus buried his body in a borrowed tomb near Jerusalem. Exactly where his spirit went after his death remains a mystery, and within that mystery lies the very nature Psalm 16:10 of his sacrifice. The Bible (at least in older translations) indicates that Jesus went into hell, but that does not answer all our questions. There are four words translated as "hell" in many Job 11:8 versions of the Bible. The Hebrew *Sheol* and the Greek *Hades* Acts 2:27 mean simply the realm of the dead without implying judgment Matthew 5:29,30 or punishment. The Greek *Gehenna* gets its name from the Valley of Hinnom, the continually burning refuse dump just outside the city of Jerusalem where trash and animal bodies were thrown. Gehenna is an analogy for a place of punishment 2 Peter 2:4 or destruction. The Greek *Tartarus* names the place of eternal punishment reserved for the Devil and his angels. The Bible says that Jesus went into Sheol or Hades, which means simply that he went into the realm of the dead and not necessarily into Gehenna or Tartarus. Many theologians think that for his death to pay for our sins, it must be in every way like ours would be. Since unrepentant sinners will be taken to Tartarus or Gehenna for punishment or destruction, Jesus, bearing our sins and condemned for them as we would be, must be taken there as well to fulfill his role as our substitute. If Sidney Carton had claimed to have gone to the guillotine for his beloved when all he did was merely lay his head on the block and withdraw it as the blade came sweeping down, one would hardly think his sacrifice complete.

The true answer to the mystery may elude us as long as we are earthbound, but rather than sidestepping such a crucial point, we might consider the following possibility: Perhaps punishment is not the primary idea behind death. Consider death as merely a tool to keep the universe clean. As we noted Romans 6:23 in chapter five, the only way to stop sin is to kill the sinner. Ezekiel 18:20 Otherwise he will continue to pollute the planet with his rebel- Romans 5:12 lion and self-will. Punishment or destruction follows death not James 1:15 by necessity or God's decree, but because man's insistence on independence from God leaves him defenseless against the hellish demonic beings bent on abducting him into Gehenna. God has nothing to do with it; he merely put the garbage out. Satan came along and stole it for his own consumption. Let's look at the Crucifixion and Resurrection with this view of death and punishment as our premise:

1 Peter 2:24

While on the cross, Jesus took on the guilt for all the sins all humanity committed from Adam to now. Because of this mass of sin, God the Father, who must by his nature reject sin utterly, had to abandon his Son. This separation of Jesus from the Father was nothing less than spiritual death of the same kind man suffers when he sins. And it caused Jesus to cry out

Matthew 27:46
Mark 15:34
Luke 23:46

in terrible anguish, "My God, My God, why have you forsaken me?" When he came to the point of physical death he cried, "Into your hands I commit my spirit," then he died. At that moment Jesus took with him the slime of our sins and all the guilt we had accumulated into the unseen realm of Hades. As Jesus passed through the gates of death, he sloughed off this mass of sin and it fell into the void of hell. Thus two things were accomplished: Humanity's sin was removed, and Jesus was made clean again from the contamination of our sin.

Psalm 16:10

Therefore God no longer had to abandon him. He could now allow his legions of angels to defend Jesus from Satan's demons because Jesus, by carrying sin into death, had done all the law required; further punishment was not a part of the deal. Now God the Father could lawfully reestablish his relationship with his Son and rescue him from death.

1 Corinthians 15:20
1 Peter 3:18
2 Corinthians 5:21
Romans 5:14

2 Corinthians 5:15

The completed cycle of Jesus' career as sketched above — life, death, and rescue from death — opened up the path by which man could return to God. Adam's sin kicked God out of man's life, which doomed him to failure at living as he was created to live. Jesus succeeded where Adam failed. Jesus submitted himself totally to God's direction, which guaranteed him success at living the life intended for humanity. It's as if Adam let in a virus that contaminated the program designed to run humanity and caused it to crash. There was no way for man to boot up again until the restart button was punched and the original, uncontaminated program reentered. But the program would run right only in a new, virus-free human. Jesus was that human. He came to us with a new bug-free program and offers us a free license to copy it into our own lives.

Romans 5:17

This means we can now claim the success of Jesus by choosing God over self, or accept the failure of Adam by choosing self over God. But there is a slight hitch. In spite of the fact that we can copy into our lives Jesus' new, virus-free program, we still have the old contaminated program to deal

Romans 7:18,21-24
Romans 8:5-8

with. It is so fused to the human hardware that we cannot detach it. That old sin nature will not let us live even a day without sinning. And when God sweeps sin out of his universe into the trash heap of hell, we are doomed to be swept out with it unless we separate ourselves from that sin nature before the broom of death catches us. We separate ourselves from our sin nature by "dying in advance" — killing its influence over our

Romans 6:11
1 Peter 2:24
2 Corinthians 4:11
Galatians 2:20
Romans 8:10,11

lives by denying it any control. The Bible calls this a death — the death of self. As we discussed in chapter four, death always means a separation. In this case it means separation from the doomed sin nature, nailing it into a coffin and giving control instead to the successful, sinless nature Jesus offers.

One would think that choosing the new nature of Jesus would exempt us from sin, but it doesn't. The old sin nature does not accept rejection well and continually distracts us by banging at the lid of the coffin. But as long as you abhor the intrusion of the sin nature and choose the perfect Christ nature as your pattern, your program, your spiritual motive power,

Romans 8:12,13

Jesus will honor your intent and take all your sins and guilt as his own. By choosing to die in advance to the domination of the sin nature, you free yourself from its doom.

Dying in advance to your sin nature does not exempt you from physical death, of course. It is a little like an insurance

Colossians 3:3,4

policy — a sort of pre-need agreement with God as to how your death will be handled. Choose the Christ nature over the sin nature now and you qualify for God's protection from Satan when you die. The contract says that if you will die to that sin nature, Jesus will take all the sin it churns out and carry the guilt into death himself. This means that you will enter physical death free of actual sin. The only reason you have to enter it at all is to rid yourself once and forever of that bothersome sin nature. Death is the only cure for it. It's got to be thrown out into the garbage. As you die, your sin nature will fall away from you, crashing and burning into the trash heap of hell as you settle into the safety of God's loving hands. And when you sit up and look around, you will find yourself sporting only the perfect nature he gave you when you chose to die in advance. But now that nature will be total. It will no longer be hampered by the continual interruption of the old sin nature. This means you will be sin-free, and God can resurrect you as he did Jesus to live in a perfect environment with him.

Those who refuse to die in advance, insisting instead on retaining their selfish nature, will go into physical death with that sin nature intact and none of their guilt removed. God will grant them the independence they demanded and leave them to themselves, utterly defenseless as they fall into the grip of Satan's demons in the darkness of Gehenna.

The Resurrection

When God's Spirit came back to Jesus in the realm of the dead, the bolted gates of death shattered like a window pane as Jesus exploded through them. Death could no more hold him than a spider web could hold an eagle. Satan's power was broken. His once fearsome sword of death was now twisted and blunted. It was the beginning of the end for Satan. He was still Lord of the Earth; Adam's choice had given him that title to hold as long as the earth lasted. But his deadlock on man's destiny was forever smashed and the days of his control over the earth were numbered. In desperation he fights on, but it is a futile and hopeless rear-guard action. He is defeated, and it is just a matter of time before he knows it.

Now that Jesus was sinless again, he could resume his role as man. God's Spirit again took up residence in Jesus and he returned immediately to earth. On the third morning after he was crucified, he re-entered his body and burst from the tomb where he had been buried.

This victorious emergence from the grave, which we know as the Resurrection, is the key event in human history. Without the Resurrection, Jesus was just another of many crucified by

Philippians 1:21

Hebrews 2:14,15
Acts 2:24

1 Corinthians 15:25,
26,54,55
Hebrews 2:14
John 12:31

Matthew 28
Mark 16:1-6
Luke 24:1-6
John 20:1-9
1 Corinthians
15:13,14

the Romans. Without the Resurrection, Christianity is just another human religion with good moral teachings and a charismatic founder, but with no real answer to humanity's dilemma. Without the Resurrection, God's plan to save humanity from Adam's sin was incomplete. We would have no way of knowing that Jesus finished his campaign successfully. Jesus had to rise again as a man to establish the pattern that we were to follow. He had to blaze the trail. He had to swim the river of death to attach a line so we could be ferried across. Without the Resurrection of Jesus there would be no victory and no hope that we would ever emerge from our own graves. The brightest words in our language are *Jesus rose from the dead.*

For several days after the Resurrection, Jesus appeared to many of his friends and followers. They were shocked, to say the least. At first they were terrified because they thought he was a ghost, but they quickly saw that he was not. He ate, drank, walked, talked, fished, cooked, and did all the common things that living humans do. He even let people touch him to prove beyond all doubt that he was real flesh and bones.

Yet, there was something different about Jesus after the Resurrection. At times he would be hard to recognize for a moment or longer. People who were with him would sometimes feel a strange but exciting thrill or burning sensation within their hearts. He would startle his friends when he suddenly appeared or disappeared without warning. His body had been changed. It was the same body he had lived in before he was crucified, but it was greatly improved. It was now a permanent, age-proof, pain-proof, and death-proof model. His body was what we call *immortal*, which means it is guaranteed to last just as long as the spirit that lives within it, which is forever. The body and spirit will never separate again.

Jesus stayed on earth only a few days after his Resurrection. He told his followers that he must leave them to prepare a place where they could come and live the same kind of immortal life they now saw him living. In the meantime, he instructed them to wait in Jerusalem where he would send a gift to comfort them in his absence. Then, as they watched, he rose into the air and vanished.

1 Corinthians 15:21,22

Mark 16:12-18

Luke 24:39-40

John 20:14-16

Luke 24:13-49

John 20:18–21:25

Mark 16:19
Luke 24:49-53
Matthew 28:16-20
John 14:2,3

Luke 24:49-51

What the Incarnation Cost God

When we back off and look at the story of Jesus from a cosmic perspective, it gives us cause for awe and wonder. Jesus was one with the Creator and Lord of the universe whose power brought into existence the galaxies, planets, light, and life. His power originated and maintains all the natural laws by which creation operates. For him to leave this exalted status and become one of his own creatures is almost unimaginable. Analogies are too weak to express it. It is something like a toymaker becoming one of his own dolls; or a novelist becoming a character in his own story; or a veterinarian becoming a spaniel; or an entomologist becoming a beetle.

John 1:1-3

You may think we are making a bigger thing of Jesus' coming than we should. After all, he was God, and whatever pain and discomfort his tenure on earth cost him, it was only temporary. Even though his tour of duty here lasted over thirty years, surely that is less than a split second by the clock of eternity. It's now done and over; he is back with God the Father, and everything is just as it was. He did a great and wonderful thing for us and we are deeply grateful, but after all is said and done, it seems to have cost him virtually nothing.

Don't be too sure of that. We have no way of knowing exactly what the Incarnation and Crucifixion cost God, but we have hints that the cost was stunning. And it may have had an eternal effect on the nature of God. To appreciate this possibility, we must make an attempt to understand something about the nature of time in relation to God. Of course, we know that time-locked creatures like ourselves cannot accurately imagine how God exists in eternity, but perhaps we can catch a dim glimmer of it. The nature of time is such that we experience a continuing sequence of moments, each following the previous as they come from the future, enter the present, and move into the past. These moments are like railway cars passing by a narrow window. The window allows us to see each car one at a time as it passes, and the car we see at any given moment represents the present. We experience the future as the part of the train yet to come, and can "see" it only in the imagination. The past consists of train cars gone by, and they exist only in

2 Peter 3:8

memory. But to God, time apparently is not strung out in a fixed sequence of past-present-future. Perhaps to him eternity is not, as we imagine it, just time extended to infinity. He is not limited to experiencing time as a succession of passing moments, but as one eternal moment that makes both future and past accessible as a present experience. He sees time not like a train of railway cars in an unalterable sequence, but like the track upon which they run. To him, eternity contains time. Past, present, and future exist simultaneously within eternity giving him access to past, present, and future at will. This concept explains how God can know the future; to him it exists already, and he need only attend to it. The beginning and the end are eternally present to him.

Using the above supposition about God and time, we can begin to see how the Incarnation may have affected him. The hours of agony Jesus experienced while on earth may be forever a part of the experience of God. The separation of Father from Son on the cross between the words, "why have you forsaken me?" and "Into your hands I commend my spirit," may hurt God even yet.

Please be aware that such thoughts as those above about the nature of God in eternity and the nature of the Godhead after the Incarnation are the result of considerable interpretation and *should not be accepted uncritically as confirmed truth*. They are presented here as a possible way of understanding a certain truth that has roots deeper than our minds can reach — that the

1 Peter 1:12

sacrifice God made for us is a cosmic wonder that inspires awe in the angels and rattled the foundations of the universe. We must not dismiss it lightly as being no big thing for God.

Questions for Discussion: Chapter 9

1. Why did Pontius Pilate execute Jesus? Why did the Jews want him killed?

2. When Jesus descended into Hades, did he also enter Gehenna?

3. If Jesus went into hell, how did he get out?

4. What is the importance of the Resurrection of Jesus?

5. What does Jesus' resurrected body show us about our own future?

6. What did the sacrifice of Jesus cost the Godhead?

7. Is Jesus still a man?

10 The Return of the Spirit

Acts 1:4

After Jesus ascended to heaven, his followers stayed together in Jerusalem where they waited for the gift he had promised them. As they waited, they must have wondered what sort of thing this gift would be. They may have thought Jesus

Acts 1:6

was about to restore to Israel the power and glory of the days when David and Solomon were kings. This is what most Jewish scholars expected of the coming Messiah. The followers of Jesus knew the gift would have something to do with

Luke 24:49

power, because he had told them so. They waited and wondered for nine days, but nothing happened.

Acts 2:1

The tenth day after Jesus ascended was a Sunday. It was also a special Jewish holiday called Pentecost, and Jerusalem

Acts 2:5

was brimming with thousands of Jews from many nations who had come to their ancient capital to celebrate. Pentecost was also called the Feast of the First Fruits or Feast of the Harvest. It was somewhat like our American Thanksgiving holiday. The people gave thanks for their crops and offered a part of them to God in gratitude. Pentecost, which means *fiftieth day*, came fifty days after the Passover Feast, the Jewish holiday that celebrates their deliverance from Egypt under Moses.

The Gift

Acts 2:1-41

On the day of Pentecost, these followers of Jesus were sitting together in a second-story room, when suddenly a deafening roar like the sound of a hurricane filled their ears. Bright darts of light shot down and glowed like tongues of fire above the heads of each disciple. The people of the city were astounded at the noise and rushed to the house to see what was happening. They were even more astounded when the disciples of Jesus came out and began to speak, because everyone in the crowd could understand them perfectly. The thousands that gathered around the disciples undoubtedly represented all the Mediterranean nations, yet each person there was able to hear at least one disciple speaking in his or her own language. The disciples were speaking to the crowd in languages they had never learned; it was the tower of Babel in reverse.

Then the bold disciple Peter, who had been one of Jesus' closest friends, stood up before the crowd and began to preach a sermon. He identified Jesus of Nazareth as the Messiah their prophets had predicted. (The word *Messiah* is translated as *Christ* in the New Testament. It means the anointed one, or the chosen one.) Peter explained the sacrifice Jesus made for them, and urged them to accept him as their substitute and demonstrate that acceptance by going through the ritual of baptism. About 3000 of his listeners did just that, and we can easily understand why. The triple miracle of wind, fire, and language was like nothing they had ever seen or heard.

But something even greater happened that day that could not be seen or heard: the Spirit of God returned. His return caused the mighty noise and the tongues of fire. His return caused the followers of Jesus to speak fluently in the languages of their hearers, and his return caused the 3000 to believe and respond.

The return of the Holy Spirit was the gift that Jesus had promised his disciples before he left the earth. On this first Pentecost after the Resurrection, God gave back to man what Adam and Eve had lost in Eden. The Spirit of God returned to fill the empty space in man's spirit and restore man to his original design. Man again became what he was created to be — a container for the life of God.

1 Corinthians 6:19
Romans 8:9

On that Pentecost morning, the followers of Jesus finally understood what God's plan to save man was all about. While the plan was unfolding, no one was in a position to see the vastness of the complete design. A single thread is not in touch with the entire fabric. For hundreds of years, students and scholars had studied tantalizing hints and glimpses in prophecies and rituals of some great event that would shine forth from Judah like a beacon to the nations, but the puzzle had remained unsolved. On this Pentecost the missing piece appeared and everything fell into place. Now it became clear that God was restoring more than just Israel's lost glory; he was restoring all humanity's lost glory. The Jews were expecting to get their own house repaired, but found that the whole neighborhood was to be renovated. Now they could see that God had chosen them as a special nation because they had a special duty — to bring the Christ to the world. Now they could understand the mysterious meanings behind the rituals and sacrifices of their religion. All these acts and symbols were veiled pictures of Jesus, who came to take on the sin that separated man from God. And when man's sin was removed, God could offer his Spirit to live again in man's cup-shaped spirit.

The Choice

To sharpen our focus before we consider this next point, let's pause and telescope two or three principles we discussed in the previous chapters. Remember that at the control center of every human is a spirit, designed as a container for the Spirit of God. God created man to be the bearer of his Spirit, just as a candle bears a flame. However, the Holy Spirit withdrew from man when man sinned by rejecting God's direction and choosing his own instead. From that point on, the empty-spirited man bumped and stumbled around the planet like a headless chicken, leaving a trail of confusion, havoc, distress, and disorder. And the worst of the matter was that man could not step back into his former relationship with God any more than a chicken could reattach its own head. Having become a sinner, man's nature was incompatible with God's nature, therefore God could no longer allow his Holy Spirit to reside in man. Neither could he allow the man to live indefinitely on his planet because his sin would eventually ruin it. God had to sentence him to death to eliminate sin from creation. Man's case seemed hopeless.

Romans 8:7

The death of Jesus solved the problem. Jesus took man's guilt, which left man legally innocent. This meant God could legitimately return his Spirit to man's spirit and restore humanity to its original design. The whole purpose of God's plan is restoration. He intends to put the universe back into the shape it was in at the end of the sixth day of creation when everything was good and perfect. God's original design for the universe is the pattern for the way things ought to be, and he doesn't intend to let a malevolent upstart like Satan force him into settling for less.

The return of the spirit on Pentecost was a giant step in the process of restoration. God's Spirit became available to everyone who voluntarily chose to open his or her life to God's direction and live under his control as man was created to live. The Spirit came first to the followers of Jesus who waited in Jerusalem, then to the 3000 who responded to Peter's sermon. He still comes into the life of everyone who chooses to become a follower of Jesus.

Put simply, the purpose of Christianity is to give you a way to become the kind of creature God intended when he made Adam and Eve. But as in the beginning, God still does not force anyone to make this choice. We are not animals or robots; we have the same right Adam and Eve had — the right to choose whether to follow Christ and accept God's Spirit or to follow Satan into banishment and death.

You might wonder why anyone would not choose to follow Jesus. Why deliberately follow Satan instead? It is safe to say that very few people deliberately follow Satan. Most who follow him do so because his way is easier or looks more inviting. And they don't really think they are following Satan, or anyone else, for that matter; they think they are doing exactly what they want to do personally, just as a rat thinks as he gorges himself on the bait that leads to the trap. Satan encourages us to think we are doing exactly what we want, and that doing what one wants is the way to happiness. He cranks out promises like a presidential candidate, offering just the right scratch for every itch. We think we are in control of our lives when we arrange things so we can do exactly what we want, but we're not really; we are under the control of those itches. We are dancing to the beat of desires, whims, obsessions, and cravings which Satan orchestrates to lure us into the jaws of his trap. The problem is that when we get into the comfortable

John 14:16,17
Romans 8:9

2 Corinthians 5:17

2 Corinthians 2:11
2 Corinthians 11:3

104

Romans 8:5

Romans 8:14

Romans 6:3-8

habit of having those cravings satisfied, we don't want things any other way. We like the idea of thinking we can run our lives in just the way we want.

But when we follow Jesus, we do just as he did and turn the wheel over to God's Holy Spirit to live our lives as we were meant to live them. We put the Spirit in control and refer all decisions to him. We give up our rights to self and give ourselves totally to God.

Soldiers Under Orders

Becoming a follower of Jesus brings such a drastic change in one's life that the Bible calls it a death — the death of the old selfish, sin-controlled self. But that death is followed immediately by the birth of a new Spirit-controlled self. It is much like the way a caterpillar must "die" to be reborn as a butterfly. This change is so drastic and such a turning point that God has given us a solemn ritual as a physical expression of it. This ritual is called baptism. Baptism is a miniature re-enactment of what happens inside ourselves when we become Christians. When one chooses to follow Jesus, the selfish sin nature he inherited from Adam is killed. That old, dead self is buried, which is enacted when the sinner is laid down in a grave of water. Then as the new Christian is raised from that grave, he re-enacts the resurrection of Jesus from his tomb. Like Jesus, he begins a new life as a new type of creature — a newborn Adam or Eve — legally sinless, filled with God's Holy Spirit, and ready to live under his direction.

There has been much controversy over baptism. Most of it centers on the question of whether or not it is really necessary. Some insist that God does not recognize the sinner's change into a Christian until the moment of baptism. Others believe that baptism is necessary, but that we cannot pinpoint it as the magic moment when God grants salvation. As long as one is in the process of conversion, God's grace covers him. Others contend that God accepts us completely at the moment we decide to accept him, and no further act of our own makes any difference. This position is the only dangerous one of the three because it tests God by asking him to stretch his grace beyond

Acts 2:41; 8:12;
8:38; 9:18;
16:15; 16:33;
18:8; 19:5

1 John 2:3-6

our willingness to obey. It is unwise to let the controversy over baptism cause one to question the need for it. The answer to arguments over when in the conversion process God gives us his Holy Spirit is not given to us. We can be curious; we can wonder; we can speculate; or we can hold opinions as long as we don't let our own thinking get in the way of doing what we are told to do. God has commanded baptism, and every conversion recorded in the New Testament is accompanied by it. Our duty is not to question but to obey.

As soldiers under God's orders, we do not have the right to pick and choose from among his commands, deciding why some are important and others expendable. Conversion means total submission to his will. To refuse baptism might indeed undo our conversion — not because baptism is necessarily the precise moment of salvation, but because refusal would show that we are more confident in our own theories about the salvation process than in God's specific direction, which is confirmed by every biblical example of conversion. Baptism is not a work by which we earn or qualify for salvation, but an act of faith by which we show the inner truth of our death to self and rebirth in Christ, and that we intend to do all his will. Why argue that baptism is "just a symbol" and therefore unnecessary? A boot camp marine might refuse the sergeant's order to polish his shoes, reasoning that shiny shoes have nothing to do with winning wars. But if he follows this philosophy when he shows up at inspection, he can expect his DI's reaction to be swift, certain, and emphatic — not because glistening shoes are vital to an efficient army, but because following orders is. Is baptism necessary or isn't it? Why take on the task of deciding that for yourself? Leave the answering of such questions to God. When to grant us his Spirit is his own business; making a sincere attempt to show our faith by obeying him in everything is ours.

Remember, however, that baptism alone will not accomplish anything for you. It is a visible image of the true thing that happens inside when you choose to follow Jesus. It is the mark of your decision to kill your sinful nature and become born again as a Christian.

A Question of Time

The Spirit returned on a given day, in a given year fairly late in the world's recorded history. Does this mean that those who lived before that day could not experience the presence of the Holy Spirit in their lives? No, it does not mean that. A number of men who lived before the day of Pentecost were specifically described as being moved by God's Spirit. Among these were Gideon, Samson, Saul, and David. In some of these instances it seems that the Holy Spirit was given in a special measure or for a special purpose, whereas for Christians living after Pentecost the Holy Spirit is clearly a continuing presence and the dynamic of their lives. However, we know that the Holy Spirit lived as totally in the lives of believers before Pentecost as well as after because it is impossible to live a godly life without him. All men and women throughout time are saved by the same medium — the blood of Christ. The sacrifice of Jesus reaches backward as well as forward to save all believers before and after his death. The gift of the Holy Spirit works the same way. God, whose foreknowledge is perfect, could see from the moment Adam sinned that Christ would die to pay the penalty for it. On the basis of that knowledge he could set all believers free from the penalty of sin and give them his Holy Spirit to enable them to live as godlike men and women.

Before the Crucifixion, the Resurrection, and Pentecost, God's plan was a mystery only hinted at in the writings of the prophets. The advantage we have in living after these events is that we know what was done for us and who lives in us.

Judges 6:34;14:6
1 Samuel
    10:10;16:13
Psalm 51:11

Romans 8:9

Romans 3:25,26
Hebrews 9:15

Questions for Discussion: Chapter 10

1. What did Jews come to celebrate in Jerusalem on the day of Pentecost?

2. What is the significance of Pentecost to Christians?

3. What is the purpose of the Holy Spirit in the lives of men and women?

4. What is the meaning of baptism?

5. Is baptism necessary to salvation?

6. Did believers who lived before Pentecost have the Holy Spirit?

11 The Body

The term *Christian* means *follower of Christ*. Jesus Christ set the standard for human behavior and showed us by his life the pattern we must follow to achieve restoration of our original pre-Fall nature. While on earth, Jesus submitted himself to God the Father, allowed God's Holy Spirit to live in him, and thus became God's body on earth. By everything he did, he showed to all creation the nature of God in heaven. But when Jesus died to become our sacrifice for sin, God no longer had a body on earth to reflect his holy nature. That is where we step in. We give him ours. The star player scored the winning points, but had to be carried from the field. Now we are called from the bench to be his substitute. We are called to replace Jesus as God's body on earth.

John 14:9,10

Jesus gave up his own rights as God in heaven and made himself available to be directed by God the Father. We follow by imitation. We give up our rights as independent, self-directed humans and make ourselves available to be directed by God's Holy Spirit. When God lives in us, we become his body on earth, just as Jesus before us was his body on earth. We step in and take Jesus' place.

1 Corinthians 12:27

Of course, God cannot express himself as fully through the lives of created beings like us as he could through the life of his own Son. All there is of God could live uncramped in the God-sized spirit of Jesus, but not in the thimble-sized spirits of fallen humans. It takes all the followers of Jesus acting together to make up the body that replaces Jesus as God's body on earth.

It might seem that becoming one of so many parts of the vast body of God means the Christian must give up his individual identity. But the opposite is true. Apart from God, we actually have no individual identity worth preserving. We are like gloves without hands inside them — useless until we are shaped and motivated by a living power within. For us to insist on being independent, to stand alone, to do it on our own, to do it "my way," is to insist on being useless and meaningless. We don't become a part of the body of God in the same way that a drop of water becomes a part of the sea. We don't merge into oblivion and cease to function as individual beings. We join God's body much like a stereo cassette joins a tape player. The connection allows us to become fully what we are meant to be. If you wish you can insist on remaining independent, but you will make no music.

Far from forcing us into a production mold, becoming believers lifts us out of the pack and makes each of us truly

Revelation 2:17

unique. God designed each person to know him in a particular way that no one else can. He can reveal something about himself to you that he can reveal to no other human on earth. That is why we are all different. Your role as a human is to show one particular facet of God to the rest of creation. His many facets are as different as snowflakes, and he designed each of us to match up with one of those facets in particular. He beams upon each believer a single ray from his unlimited spectrum, giving each of us a hue that differs from all others. Your assignment as a Christian is to pick up that beam and reflect it. Our search for meaning and satisfaction, our attempts to "find ourselves" are all efforts to find that beam God wants to shine on us. All believers together when properly turned toward God, reflect to the world a dazzling image of his splendor and character.

The Body of Christ

1 Corinthians
12:12- 27
Romans 12:5-8
Ephesians 4:11-16

The New Testament explains the uniqueness of the believer by telling us that he is not like a mere cell in the body of Christ, but like one of its organs or limbs. Each has a unique place and function. Some believers are the body's eyes; they see needs and keep watch. Others are arms and hands, laboring in the day-to-day work of the body. The body's mouth are those believers who speak and teach God's message and instructions. The feet are missionaries who carry the good news to others, telling them how man can now overcome the finality of death. The head of the body is Christ himself, and the Holy Spirit living within each member gives it life. The New Testament calls this body of believers the church.

Ephesians 1:22,23;
4:15,16
1 Corinthians 3:16

Like any living body, the church must take certain measures in order to stay alive and healthy. Members of the church must meet together regularly to keep the body breathing and in working shape. Meeting regularly helps both Christians and non-Christians to identify the church, making the body of Christ more visible to everyone. Meeting enables Christians to unite and plan their mission to share what they have found with those who are still looking. When church members meet, qualified teachers instruct them in the ways of living as God-like beings. Together they offer praise and give thanks to God, expressing the joy of being members of God's body in the special magic of song.

Acts 20:7
Hebrews 10:25

Celebrating the Body

1 Corinthians
11:23-26
Acts 20:7

Matthew 26:26

1 Corinthians
10:16,17

At the center of the assembled church's activity is a sacred memorial service called the Lord's Supper or Communion. Christians celebrate Communion regularly as a visible enactment of their membership in the body of Christ. This solemn celebration involves eating bread and drinking wine or grape juice to give us a graphic picture of our identification with Jesus. The bread is taken as Christ's body which was sacrificed on the cross. When Christians eat a piece of this bread, they keep the body of Christ alive. His body that was killed on the cross becomes one with the living body of each Christian. The Crucifixion gave us life, but it left God without a body on earth through which to express his nature. So the Christian offers his own as a substitute. It's as if your big brother's car was totalled in the process of rushing you to the hospital for a life-saving operation, so you give him yours as a permanent loan. The ritual eating of the bread is the believer's commitment to take the place of Jesus as the body in which God now lives.

Matthew 26:27,28
1 Corinthians 10:16

Christians complete the ritual by drinking a small quantity of wine or grape juice. This drink is taken as the blood that

Leviticus 17:11

drained from the body of Jesus as he hung on the cross. The Bible tells us that life is in the blood. When Christians drink the ritual wine, they take his spilled life from the base of the cross and pour it into their own bodies. Thus the image is complete; the life of Christ lives on in a body on earth. The church is that body. By eating bread and drinking wine, Christians show that they accept their assignment to take up where Jesus left off. They become what Jesus was when he lived on the earth — a body that contains the life of God.

These enactments show us that life in the church is vital to a Christian. Believers must express their Christianity visibly to each other and to the world by interacting with fellow Christians as a united body. By coming together regularly to participate in worship and fellowship, Christians both support and draw strength from each other. A Christian can no more

John 15:5,6

survive apart from the church than a hand can survive separated from the body.

Not everyone immediately finds church attendance such a positive experience. Many who consider themselves Christians choose to hold aloof from the assembly, insisting, "I can live just as good a Christian life without attending church as I could if I went every Sunday." Such people usually find the rituals boring, the music bad, the preacher out of touch, the crying babies distracting, and especially, the church full of hypocrites. Of course, it is true that the church is not all it should be, but

Matthew 5:13-16

the world needs the church in spite of its shortcomings. And it is the duty of Christians to keep it functioning by their attendance and participation. An imperfect church is better than no church at all.

It may be true that one can live a good life without attending church assemblies, but those who make the claim miss the point of church. Church attendance is not designed to be a punishing experience — something we have to do to pay our dues to God. It is surprising how many Christians slip into the habit of thinking of church attendance as a burdensome duty — an exercise of sacrifice, discipline, and willpower — like the discipline of a released prisoner who must appear regularly before his parole board. When Christians enter the church doors with such a mindset, something is out of kilter, and more often than not, the problem is in the pew rather than the pulpit. Members brought up with television often come to church expecting to be more entertained than taught. The minds of many Christians are so focused on the material world that they lack a deep interest in the things of God. In fact, there is now such a wide split between the standards of secular society and the church that the church has been made to look like an anachronism, out of touch with reality and unable to keep pace with sophisticated modern thinking about social issues, entertainment, the arts, science, and technology. Involvement in church may seem a little embarrassing to those whose focus has been drawn deeply into the current secular mindset.

Philippians 4:8

Whatever one focuses on becomes his life. Whatever has your attention has you.

We can come to know the church and reap its benefits only if we plunge into it without reservation. In nineteenth century Scottish author George MacDonald's story *The Golden Key*, the heroine Tangle finds that the trail of her quest has led her to a deep, black hole in the ground. "But there are no stairs," she said to her guide. He answered, "You must throw yourself in. There is no other way." If you expect to get anything out of church, you must throw yourself in. You must attend regularly, participate in its activities, partake of its rituals, work to accomplish its mission, and share the joys and pains of your fellow members. Do these things and you will find that involvement ceases to be a duty and becomes the major center of your life and fulfillment.

1 John 1:7

Nothing can replace the fellowship, support, love, and warmth that Christians can find with each other. The bonds you establish with your Christian friends can become much stronger, deeper, and more rewarding than friendships with non-Christians can ever be. One Christian expressed it like this: "When I attend some church activity like a youth meeting or a study group, I feel much closer to Christians in that group that I barely know — and even to those in the group that I have not yet met — than to non-Christian friends I have known and worked with for many years."

Is the Church Full of Hypocrites?

It would be dishonest to tell the new Christian that he will inevitably experience this sort of love and warmth the first few times he crosses the church threshold. Many church members do not know how to welcome new Christians. Many have the desire but lack the courage or the social skills to converse comfortably with a stranger. Others simply are not sensitive to the presence of outsiders. They are so caught up in the interchange of existing fellowship that they overlook their duty to expand the fellowship circle. Still others are mere churchgoers, and not committed Christians at all. Long before the church service ends, their thoughts are already on the roast in the oven, the football game, the lake, or the afternoon nap, for which they may be already practicing. A visitor in need of a friendly welcome and an outstretched hand is not their concern; it is the preacher's.

Encountering such attitudes and failures can be painfully disillusioning to the new believer aching to be enfolded into the fellowship of caring Christians. As he stands amid the chatter and banter of shared love with scarcely a howdy or a handshake coming his way, his new-found faith may begin to evaporate.

Attitudes and failures such as these are unfortunate and need to be corrected. But it's also true that many newcomers don't give church members a real chance to welcome them. While the last amen is still echoing, they make a laser line for the door, then complain, "That was the coldest church I ever saw; no one even spoke to me." Newcomers to the church need to take their first step toward spiritual maturity right at the threshold of their new life in Christ, and be prepared to exercise a little forgiveness and patience toward their Christian brothers and sisters. They should make it a point to hang around for a while after the services, making themselves available to the deeper, more caring Christians that can be found in almost every church. Those who really want their boats to sail will expose them to the best winds.

But newcomers to the church have such high expectations that they are often shocked and affronted to find that church members have human weaknesses. All too often they turn away in disgust and pronounce the outsider's perennial judgment on the church: "They're all just a bunch of hypocrites."

This criticism of the church surely wins by a landslide as the most widely used excuse for staying away. And it seems that each critic who utters it thinks he has come up with an original insight. Certainly the church is full of hypocrites. Hypocrites are everywhere else; why shouldn't the church have its share? But hypocrites no more invalidate a church than weeds invalidate a garden. Gold is no less valuable because it has an imitator called fool's gold. Indeed, the very fact that the church attracts hypocrites is a strong indication that it must have something real that is worth imitating.

This persistent criticism of the church shows that most outsiders misunderstand its true nature. They expect Christians to be immune to the temptations and cured from the sins that infect society at large. But as one popular advice columnist put it, "A church is not a showplace for saints; it's a hospital for sinners." The church is not a place for people who are better than the rest of society; it is a place for people who have been forgiven.

On the other hand, it is true that the effect of the authentic Christian life is to make the believer grow more and more like Christ. This means the Christian must continually be cleaning out areas of his life that are given to sin and placing them under the control of the Spirit. And this is not easy because the self is still selfish. That "I want what I want when I want it" nature we inherited from Adam is still with us, and it kicks and screams at the idea of giving up any control to the Spirit of God. It will not and cannot submit to the Spirit. Therefore, the Christian, saddled with a nature that is in opposition to God, must thwart that nature by acting according to God's standards instead of doing what his fallen nature demands. He must behave as he knows he should instead of as he wants. He must act better than he feels like acting. He must obey the road signs, stop lights, and center stripes instead of yielding to that inner urge to floorboard it.

In the general view of the outside world, this acting better

Matthew 13:24-30

Matthew 9:12,13

1 Peter 3:18

Romans 8:7

Romans 8:13
Colossians 3:5-10
1 Peter 2:11,12

than one feels is the essence of hypocrisy. Most people today seem to think that honest behavior means always saying what you think and acting as you feel. We can imagine the misery of living in a world where no one put any restraints on their words or feelings. But the Christian knows that since our feelings are often manipulated by that old, selfish, fallen nature, they are unreliable guides for behavior. He recognizes that there are objective standards for human behavior and attempts to follow them even against the protest of his feelings. In this sense, it is not hypocritical to feel one way and act another. It is certainly hypocritical for one to pretend to be better than he is in order to win adulation, position, or advantage. It is hypocritical to wear one sort of behavior for presentation to the public, and another more selfish and unrestrained behavior in private. It is hypocritical to wear a facade of good behavior with no intention of changing the bad behavior behind the mask.

But it is not hypocritical to act from principle rather than feelings. Behavior according to principle instead of preference shows God that you are choosing his will over your own. The behavior is the result of the choice. It gives the signal for the Holy Spirit to move in and retake territory from enemy occupation.

A Beacon for Society

The church has many flaws, and no doubt it deserves much of the criticism that comes its way. But the flaws and criticism do not invalidate its purpose, and most of its critics know that. Their criticism is often a camouflage thrown up to deflect attention from the fact that they want to avoid commitment.

Matthew 5:14
Acts 13:47
Philippians 2:15

But somewhere beneath the frenetic stream of their conscious thought lies the realization that the church is an island of solidity in a sea of change and chaos. They ignore the church when their boat skims along with a full sail on a smooth sea, but when the lightning flashes and the waves wash over the deck, they head for the shining beacon of that island. People may deride the church as useless, out of touch, out of fashion, or hypocritical, but they turn to it first in times of need and trouble. When marital problems threaten to break the home apart, the first choice for counseling is usually a minister. When the son or daughter is caught in the web of addiction, the church is a primary choice for help and direction. When the diagnosis is terminal, it's the minister who is called for help in coping with the shock, and for assurance of life beyond the grave. When financial crises threaten the family with hunger or loss of home, the first number dialed is that of the church.

The world needs the Christian church, and society in general knows it. The church must be kept alive and healthy to remain a beacon of solidity to a floundering world, and that means someone must commit to active involvement in its life and programs. To borrow the words of a late American politician: "If not you, who? If not now, when?"

Questions for Discussion: Chapter 11

1. What does it mean to be God's body on earth?

2. Does becoming a Christian force one into a mold so that he or she loses individuality?

3. Can one be a Christian without attending church assemblies?

4. What is the meaning of the church's communion service?

5. Why do outsiders claim the church is full of hypocrites? Is this criticism valid?

6. Is it hypocrisy to act better than one feels? Why?

7. Is the church important to society as a whole? Why?

12 Why Do I Still Hurt?

Observing the chaotic state of the world today might lead one to conclude that something must have gone wrong with God's plan for restoration. If the return of the Spirit is supposed to patch things up between God and man and restore the conditions that existed before the Fall, God had better take the plan back to the drawing board; it's not working. This world we're living in is hardly the Garden of Eden. The pages of your morning newspaper are crowded with reports of thievery, murder, sickness, hate, greed, cruelty, hunger, death, and other horrors that befell unfortunate victims within the past twenty-four hours. "Convenience store robberies rise 50%;" "Man found slain beside highway;" "Food airlift too little, too late for thousands in Africa;" "Apparent murder suicide leaves family of four dead;" "Freeway accident leaves pedestrian paralyzed;" "Woman assaulted, tortured in apartment;" "Civic leader succumbs to long illness;" "Nine-year-old girl found slain in vacant lot." All around us the world groans with tragedy and pain.

These grim headlines might seem more understandable to Christians if the tragedies they reported happened only to nonbelievers. But that is not the case. Sincere Christians trying their best to live under the Spirit's control suffer the same kinds of debilitating blows as their unchurched neighbors. And even the most dedicated Christians still have sin wreaking havoc in their own lives. In spite of their resolve, they find themselves committing the very sins they try hardest to avoid.

No doubt you have felt the bruising punches of pain and tragedy yourself — perhaps enough to wonder whether you will ever recover. And whether or not you are a Christian, you know that death is lurking in the shadows of the future like a thug in a dark alley, waiting to keep a certain rendezvous that only it knows. Even with the Spirit of God in your life, you do not suddenly find yourself in control of your mind or body. The same old temptations still tug at your senses and the same old weaknesses still sap your resolve. Being a Christian doesn't seem to make the road any smoother or the grass any greener, and you wonder, "Why not? If God in Adam made him perfect, why doesn't God in me make me perfect?" Christians must understand the answer to this question, because the very existence of pain and suffering is a hurdle that trips up too many potential believers. And the continued experience of pain in the lives of believers causes many to have second thoughts. Sooner or later, almost everyone asks, "How can a good God allow so much pain and tragedy to run rampant in his world?" Many reason that either he is not good and will not eradicate pain, or he is not all-powerful and cannot eradicate it. Either way they have a god who is not worth believing in, so they turn away and step off the cliff into atheism.

Why Things Are Not Right

The choice between a weak god and a cruel or indifferent god is not the only alternative available. There are rational explanations for pain that vindicate both the goodness and the omnipotence of God. The first of these is that God is still honoring the choice Adam made in Eden, and we are still saddled with the effects of that choice. God made Adam free to choose whether he would obey his creator, thus maintaining the perfect order of the created world; or obey Satan, and bring evil and death into it. Adam made the wrong choice — the choice that allowed the invasion of evil — so evil must stay with us as long as the world is inhabited by Adam's race.

Romans 5:12

If God had stepped in and taken away the evil results of Adam's sin, he would have invalidated Adam's freedom to choose. If having a free choice means anything at all, it must mean the bad can be chosen as well as the good. Had God hovered over Adam with a magic wand poised to correct Adam's errors every time he made bad choices, Adam's freedom would have been a sham. He would not have been a true human at all, but a slave to God's will — a puppet or a robot. Suffering and death are with us because Adam was not a robot; he was free to choose, and he made the wrong choice.

Jesus died, not to undo what Adam freely chose, but to give us a way to remove ourselves from the doom of Adam's choice. Now we can make the choice to get God's Spirit back into our lives, thus restoring our relationship to him; but he can't give us a choice that runs counter to the one Adam already made for the race as a whole. Adam's pivotal position as progenitor of the human race gave him the power to determine the nature of the world and mankind from his time forward; therefore, his choice stands. The world is infested with evil, and we must live with sin-damaged natures.

Romans 5:14

As you can see, God faced what seems at first a virtually impossible dilemma. On the one hand, he had to honor the choice of Adam by leaving the results of it lying as they fell. On the other hand, he had to give Adam's descendants their own freedom of choice in order to validate their humanity. He could not change humanity's fallen condition without denying Adam's freedom, but he could not leave us unalterably locked into that fallen condition without denying our freedom.

2 Peter 1:4

God's solution to the dilemma was to offer man a new unfallen nature *in addition to* the existing fallen nature that man already had. This would not break any rules or go back on any promises because the fallen nature we inherited from Adam would still be intact; Adam's choice would stand. But by making his Holy Spirit available to live in man, man could choose to have a pre-Fall nature as well. We can choose to have a Spirit-controlled nature as our own just like Adam and Eve before the Fall, but unlike them, we have it in addition to, not instead of our inherited fallen sin natures.

Romans 7:14-25

Even though as Christians we have chosen to live under the control of the Spirit, we are stuck with that rebellious fallen nature we inherited from Adam, and that nature is our major source of grief and misery. Like a cornered animal, it fights our efforts to live and act according to the new nature we have chosen. It kicks and screams and begs and pleads. It enlists the unfair support of our desires and senses and pride. With noble effort and sincere conviction, we may decide once and for all to sweep out the sinful impulses, evil intentions, selfish attitudes, and illicit desires that have nested in our minds so God's Spirit can come in and take over completely. But the old nature won't let it happen. A fallen race such as ours is too weakened by sin and too much under its influence to choose to live under the new nature with decisive finality. As we find when we make new year's resolutions or determine to diet or quit smoking, our well-meaning resolve evaporates all too quickly even without the pressure of exceptional temptation. Our wills are simply too feeble and our minds too dulled even to make the decision that would strengthen our weak wills and clear our dull minds. We have found the well that will quench our thirst, but our buckets are too leaky to draw the water. The rope that will lift us from the pit is easily within our reach, but we haven't the grip to hold on to it. We have in hand a coupon for free eyeglasses that would cure our nearsightedness, but we can't see clearly enough to find the optometrist's office. The remedy for our fallen condition is available, but our fallen condition leaves us too weak to take advantage of it. In spite of our best efforts to tame our wills to ignore the tug of temptation and live totally under the Spirit's control, our senses rebel and go on grabbing for the gusto.

Romans 8:5-11

One Christian, describing the internal battle between the Holy Spirit and his own fallen nature said, "It seems like I have these two dogs fighting continually inside my mind." When asked which of these dogs generally won the fight, he answered, "Whichever I feed the most." And so it is. Eventually one dog will grow dominant over the other and control the Christian's life. The dominant nature will be the one he pets, encourages, feeds, and gives the most attention.

Walking Battlefields

Many new Christians come to Christ without understanding that they are about to become walking battlefields. They are shocked and dismayed at the unexpected resistance to their sincere efforts to follow Jesus — from both without and within themselves. They come to him expecting a functional perfection to descend on them much as the dove descended on Jesus at his baptism. They expect somehow to be lifted out of the morass that entraps fallen humanity into a life of perpetually inflated tires and endless green lights.

Matthew 16:24-26

Many popular evangelists win their great followings by playing on such expectations. They tell their audiences that the Christian life is one of abundant possessions, abundant money, and abundant good times. But the Bible plainly tells us that the opposite is true: the authentic Christian life is often one of difficulty and persecution. Why? Because Satan is still the lord of the earth, which is another result of Adam's choice that cannot be changed until the end. Satan's philosophy dominates the thinking of the majority. As in the beginning when he tempted Eve, he still urges us to elevate our individual selves as supreme and rebel against authority. We hear it all around us: "I gotta be me"; "Everyone must decide what is right for himself"; "Nobody's gonna tell *me* what to do!"

Matthew 5:11
1 Timothy 3:12
Luke 4:5,6
Ephesians 6:12
1 John 5:19

1 Corinthians 2:14

Resistance to this programmed mindset of the herd will always mean isolation and hostility. People who advocate freedom to do one's own thing do not tend to include the freedom to assert that certain things are right and others wrong. Just as eyes accustomed to darkness cannot tolerate light, a world following the lies of Satan cannot tolerate one who holds to absolute truth. The hostility of unbelievers stems from their innate but stifled sense that the Christian's way is right. They attack Christianity because it judges their behavior and makes them feel guilty. They do what muddy little boys do when a girl in a clean white dress walks by.

Matthew 13:19
Ephesians 6:12
1 Peter 5:8

Christians often encounter more obstacles than unbelievers because Satan steps up the attack when one commits to Christ. He hammers and shakes and prods new believers in an all-out effort to derail them before they get on track.

1 John 1:8

Christians need to understand that living with an inherited fallen nature in a fallen world, they cannot expect to live perfect lives. But they can learn to live better lives, step by step, until the new Christ nature comes to be their controlling influence. When we become Christians and invite the Spirit back into our lives, he begins to help us (as much as we let

Philippians 3:12-14 him) make gradually better choices and take continually better steps that lead us toward the perfection Adam and Eve enjoyed before the Fall. The Spirit leads us *toward* perfection, but in this life we never reach it. That Adamic sin nature holds us back. A few people seem to become very good as they learn to follow the Spirit's leading, but no fallen human ever reaches the point where he can live a perfect life in this fallen world.

How to Become Perfect

So what is the point of having the Holy Spirit in our lives at all if his presence does not keep us from sinning? It is sin that separates man from God to begin with, so if his return does not put the brakes on sin, how are things improved? To take the question a step deeper, how can the Holy Spirit even stay in a life that continues to sin? As we showed in chapter five, God does not tolerate sin because sin is incompatible with his nature. He got out of Adam and Eve because they sinned, but now he offers to come back into the lives of Christians even though they have this sin nature that keeps them belching out sin like the exhaust pipe of an oil-burning clunker. Why? Has God given up on the ideal of a perfect universe? Has he decided that absolute goodness is too rigid an ideal, that he needs to back off a bit and be a little more flexible and tolerant? Has he decided that a few minor sins here and there are really not all that serious, and will really not hurt anything? Certainly not! We must stand sinless in his eyes before he can offer us his Holy Spirit. And this brings us back to the center of the dilemma; we are not sinless. We cannot behave perfectly because of our old, inherited sin nature.

2 Corinthians 5:21 The answer to the dilemma is in the fact that Jesus traded places with us when he went to the cross. He took our sins and carried them to the cross to make us sinless, and in return gave us his perfection to claim as our own. God honors this trade.

Romans 8:1,2
1 Peter 2:24 When he looks at a Christian, he sees only the sinless nature which Christ gives him and accepts the sinner as if he were perfect. And on the basis of that trade, the Christian *is* perfect; he is legally but not functionally perfect. He has the perfection of Christ to hold before the judge even though the old sin

nature is snorting and burrowing beneath the surface. God can recognize Christians as perfect because the trade gives them an automatic purifying system that non-Christians don't have. It is as if Jesus, after his death, laid a sewer line from earth to hell. When a Christian momentarily fails to follow the Spirit and commits a sin, Jesus siphons it off and dumps it through this pipeline into hell, the garbage heap outside the universe. At the same time, he pumps his own perfect nature into the Christian's life. This continual draining of sin and influx of perfection keeps the Christian perfect in the eyes of God. This undeserved recognition of the Christian as perfect is what the Bible calls grace.

1 John 1:7-9

Romans 11:6
1 Timothy 1:9

Is God Being Fair with Us?

The idea may enter your head that God is not being altogether fair with us. We are saddled with the results of Adam's folly through no fault of our own. Adam committed the sin but we must suffer the consequences. His mistake made us what we are — ruined us as perfect, Godlike creatures — and we had no say in the matter. Is that fair? We really have no right to ask the question because this is not our universe; it is God's. It's his game, his field, and his ball; we are just the players. He doesn't owe us a seat on the rules committee. He doesn't have to listen to our opinions on fairness as if we had a right to equal input on how his universe should be run. He could have discarded us like an artist throwing out a damaged painting, and started over with a blank canvas. Since he has chosen to let us live sin-diminished lives in a world of pain and tragedy, we have no cause for complaint. He made us, and we are his to do with as he will.

Job 38:1-4

However, God is not indifferent to our plight. He is fully aware that we are helpless victims of forces beyond our control — that the decisions of others have given us a fallen nature we did not personally choose. But we must remember that he did give us a solution. He did not just walk away from us like a child from a broken toy and leave us the crippled victims of fate. Instead, he gave us a way to make a choice that is the antidote to Adam's choice. Adam chose to follow Satan and

John 3:16

brought evil into a world of good. Now we can choose to follow Christ and bring good into a world of evil. Choosing Christ does not exempt us from living with the evil we inherited from Adam, but it allows God to recognize us as innocent in spite of it.

Romans 8:18-23 Although the world groans with pain and tragedy, God keeps it turning and allows the population to increase because he knows the end is worth the agony. Our few years in the arena with our adversary may leave us broken and scarred, but our very worst pains will be swallowed completely by the eternity of bliss that awaits the Christian.

Reject these answers to the existence of pain, and pain may deflect you into atheism. But you will find no answers for it there. Instead, you will find that pain hurts even worse without God. Christians feel the full impact of pain just as unbelievers do, but it does not permanently devastate them because they can look beyond it and trust God's promise to bring things right in the end.

The unbeliever does not have this comfort. To him pain is nothing less than tragic because it is an unavoidable blight on the only life he has. It's a cloud in his sky that threatens to rain out his game. Since he denies that there is life after death, he must try to build his heaven here and now. He devotes his few years to the piling up of all the pleasures and comforts he can afford. But it doesn't work, because he can't shut out the threat of disaster. The shadow of some pain either present or pending dulls the glow of every pleasure. Some wave of misfortune is sure to wash away his sand castle. The good times may come, but he knows they can't last. Sooner or later they will be ended by a doctor's diagnosis, an ambulance, a termination notice, a car crash, a tax collector, or a mortician. Like a butterfly dodging hailstones, he may think himself safe for the moment, but as he escapes one gotcha he moves into the path of another. The unbeliever travels a bumpy road with broken guardrails and washed out bridges.

And it leads him to a dead end.

Turning Pain Against Its Source

Many believers think that at least some of their pain and tragedy is inflicted by God. We hear them say things like, "God took our little child from us," either angrily blaming him for the loss or passively accepting it as his will for them. But God is never *the source* of pain or trouble. Death is never his will. Death and pain are blights on God's universe, and he detests them as such. He created the world trouble free and intended it to remain that way. Man invited pain into the world when he sinned. However, since pain is now with us, God has found ways to use it to achieve his purposes.

Hebrews 12:5-11
Revelation 3:19
Proverbs 3:11,12

God often uses pain to drive us toward him. When things are going well we tend to settle into a self-satisfied state and ignore our need for God. Like a driver on a smooth, straight road, we tend to fall asleep at the wheel, which is often fatal. Our diligence to duty gets sluggish and our sensitivity to God's will gets dulled without obstacles on which to exercise them.

In his book *The Horse and His Boy*, C.S. Lewis tells the story of a youth named Shasta and his friend Aravis. These two young people were on their horses, riding hard to warn the king of an invading army. They thought they were riding as fast as they could, but their present pace would not get them to the king in time. So the great lion Aslan (who is the Christ figure in these stories) suddenly appeared to them as a threatening wild beast. He frightened the horses and raked his claws across the back of Aravis to get them moving faster. It worked. The fright spurred them into a burst of speed that made the difference. Fear and pain accomplished what duty could not.

Job 23:10
1 Peter 1:6,7

God also uses pain as metal workers use fire on ore. It burns out all that is worthless and melts down what is pure to be shaped into something beautiful. God allows us to endure pain because he loves us too much to tolerate anything in our lives that is not good and eternal.

Ephesians 6:12

God is not the author of pain; it is with us solely because of the activity of Satan. A swarm of Satan's invisible angels works at us all the time, luring us to follow our own desires into traps of trouble and calamity. When we break away and

Job 1:9-12

chase after this bait, God may withdraw some of the angelic

Psalm 125:2

secret service protection assigned to guard Christians. They stand back and let in just enough of Satan's forces to inflict the necessary dosage of pain to wake us up and get our eyes back on the road.

Romans 5:3,4

Romans 8:18

When the Christian understands the source and purposes of pain, it loses much of its punch. It ceases to be a blight that ruins his life or destroys his happiness. The darkness doesn't bother him so much because he knows the sun is just over the horizon and about to rise.

Romans 14:8

2 Corinthians 5:5-8

Philippians 3:20

In a sense, the Christian lives in paradise in spite of the bruising blows of adversity. When he becomes a believer, the borders of heaven expand to include him. He is annexed. Christians on earth form a colony of heaven and have all the rights of citizenship. They are subject to God's laws and live under his protection; they just don't yet live on the mainland.

Ephesians 1:13,14

2 Corinthians 5:1-5

The Bible explains this foretaste of heaven by telling us that the Holy Spirit is an earnest — a sort of down payment or deposit with the promise that the full sum will be paid when the Christian leaves the colony and comes to live on the mainland. We cannot experience the full impact of the Holy Spirit in our lives because of our sin-dulled minds and fallen natures. But the dim perception of his presence and the joy that comes from what control we allow him gives us a sample of the shipment before the full delivery.

Our bodies may wear down from the incessant pounding of the earth's evil, but our spirits, united with God's, live above it all in the exhilarating atmosphere of heaven. Life on earth is the foreword; at death the first chapter begins. Life is "on your mark, get set." At death the starting gun sounds and we go for the gold.

Questions for Discussion: Chapter 12

1. Are the lives of Christians more pain-free than those of nonbelievers?

2. If God is good and all-powerful, why doesn't he eradicate pain?

3. If God took all pain from the world, what would that mean in terms of man's freedom?

4. Does the Holy Spirit in the lives of Christians make them perfect?

5. Does God see Christians as perfect? Why?

6. When a Christian sins, does that destroy his or her relationship with God?

7. Does God cause pain? How does he use pain?

13 Paradise Regained

You would think that men and women trapped in a fallen world and stuck with a fallen nature would eagerly long for the day when God takes them away from it all to live in a perfect heaven. A few do, but most do not. We find it difficult to muster up a real desire for a heaven we haven't seen and cannot clearly imagine. No doubt, our lack of enthusiasm stems in part from simple fear. We naturally fear death. Even with the assurance that God's hand will lead us safely through the shadow, it isn't easy to anticipate the passage. The chasm is solidly bridged and the guide trustworthy, but that doesn't cure our vertigo. But mainly we don't long for heaven because what most of us know of it simply doesn't appeal to us. The images of heaven we have in our minds don't seem to match up all that well with our deepest longings. It's like being invited to a chamber music concert when what we really wanted was to go to the ball game.

Revelation 21

Are these ideas we have about heaven accurate? The heavenly city described in the book of Revelation is truly magnificent — massive, golden, jeweled, impregnable, and shimmering with the glory of God's presence. But is the apostle John giving us a literal description of heaven or a symbolic picture of its perfection?

And what about the life we will live in that city? Do we imagine it accurately? Most of us share common ideas we have picked up from paintings and cartoons — static figures clad in halos and gowns, reclining dreamily on soft clouds while strumming away on golden harps or singing an endless hymn of praise in a celestial choir. And many assume we will be pure spirits in heaven. They have trouble imagining these mammal-like bodies with all their natural physical functions entering a heaven of spiritual perfection.

Do We Really Desire Heaven?

Most of us, if we are honest with ourselves, must admit that these common ideas of heaven are not very appealing. The heavenly city is undoubtedly magnificent, but it seems more like a showplace to look at than a home to live in. To spend eternity sitting around on cloudy cushions or in perpetual song may seem peaceful, but we can hardly help thinking it might get boring after a while. Floating around in the vaporous form of a pure spirit might be great fun at first, but after the novelty wore off, most of us would want our old, solid bodies back. We would miss touching, tasting, and having an apparatus capable of doing things. (There are strong indications in the New Testament that one of the tortures of demons is that they have no bodies in which to live and function. They seemed always to be looking for bodies to possess. They were so desperate that even pigs' bodies would do if they could not find a human host.)

Matthew 8:28-32

In spite of these uninviting mental pictures of heaven that most Christians share, all insist it is where they want to go when they die. Of course, there is not much else they can say; the choice is pretty limited. They can't stay on earth forever (which might be the first choice of most of us) because it is going to be destroyed, so it's either a dull heaven or a hot hell. Naturally, they choose heaven, but perhaps without real enthusiasm. It's like marrying the wealthy widow to avoid facing bankruptcy.

It's not that we don't appreciate what God is offering us; we think it's right neighborly of him to ask us to come live in his place since ours is so messed up and marked for demolition. But it all seems a little much — a little too fancy for ordinary folks like us. It's too much like visiting in the home of a rich aunt where you always have to dress your Sunday best, sit up straight, keep your feet clean, say "please" and "thank you, ma'am" and be careful about wiping your nose.

What most of us would really like is to have strong, splendid, healthy, flesh-and-blood bodies built like Greek gods or goddesses. We would like to have important things to do and exciting challenges to meet. We would like a place where we could bask in the sun and go for a dunk in an idyllic swimming hole, then dry off by running through the shade of a cool, deep woods without stickers or poison ivy.

Many of us — though we don't talk about it and like to pretend it is not important — find the idea of heaven unappealing because we think we will lose our sexuality. We enjoy being sexual creatures, and are a little disappointed (maybe more than just a *little*) by hints that sex may be an aspect of our humanness that we will be without in heaven.

But if paradise is to be restored, our unfallen, unashamed sexuality may be restored as well. If not, we can be sure that God will supply us with something as good or better. The core longing behind the sexual impulse will be satisfied, and the joy of satisfying that longing will *not* leave us wishing for our days on earth.

Looking for Eden

We know what most people would like to have in heaven because we can see what they like to have on earth. Most of our pursuits in life are actually misguided searches for paradise. Our trips to the beach or the mountains; our swimming pools, speedboats, health spas, and country clubs; our clamor for fame, wealth, or success in our careers; our craving for pleasure; our efforts to make little palaces of our homes are all attempts to satisfy longings we can't quite identify. We are trying to find peace, rest, belonging, satisfaction, significance, and fulfillment.

These deep, restless yearnings are what make us so vulnerable to Satan. What we are actually searching for is the real paradise we were meant to have, but we have never seen a real paradise and don't know how to satisfy these persistent longings. So Satan shoves before our eyes cheap but glittering imitations of the realities we are seeking. He urges us toward immediate delight for our senses, shortcuts to making our selves seem important, and temporary means of making our lives comfortable or seemingly secure. His message is that we can have it all here and now — no need to sit around longing for an iffy and maybe slice of pie in the sky by and by. Why resist all the world's delicious temptations on the promise of an insipid heaven where you will be without most of what you really enjoy? What Satan offers is short-lived and shallow, but it obscures our vision of the real object of our longings. He knows that if we think enough about houses, security, and gold, we will forget about heaven, eternity, and God.

Satan distracts us for a moment, but the glamour of his substitutes quickly fades and the old longing remains, as strong as ever. The childhood toy you wanted so badly you could taste it from Thanksgiving to Christmas was in a corner gathering dust before the new year. The dream house you had pictured and planned for years seemed boxy and commonplace before you had lived in it six months. Nothing the world can offer satisfies the longing because we are looking for something that was lost before we were born. We are looking for Paradise — for Eden. With our lips we dutifully ask for the heaven of our misinformed imagination, but in our hearts we yearn for the Eden of Adam and Eve. When we think of the paradise they lost, the mixed sense of nostalgia and desire is sometimes overwhelming. It is no wonder that our hearts beat faster when the scented breezes of Eden caress our thoughts; Eden is where we belong. We were created to live there, and our hearts are yearning for home.

We should not be too quick to write off Eden as a loss. When we look a little deeper into the book of Revelation, we find that God is planning to remake heaven and earth. Whether this means he is intending to make another universe as he made this one, or whether the one we have is to be remodeled, we can't say. Whether he uses existing atoms or creates an all new set is unimportant. It hardly matters whether the dents are to be hammered out or the parts replaced; the point is that in the long range plan there is a heaven and an earth which will exist after the event we call the end of time.

Revelation 21:1-5

Restoring the Original Plan

Why does God tell us that he is going to remake the earth? Of what possible use will it be after we are taken to heaven? He will remake it for the same reason that a man remakes his home after a tornado hits it; or that a ruler rebuilds his bombed-out country after a war. Obviously, God still has a use for the earth, and it will have been too severely damaged for a mere patchwork job. He is going to burn away all the blight and ruin and refurbish it from scratch or take the original plans and rebuild on another lot. Like a gardener who burns the dead grass from his lawn before replanting in the spring, God will utterly destroy the earth and make it over as he meant it to be in the beginning. The earth was originally created to be perfect, and to be the home of man. It seems that God's original intent is not to be thwarted. A good and omnipotent God cannot allow a creature like Satan to ruin permanently a creation that has been pronounced good. Apparently he intends to see that the universe rights itself and stays on its original course.

Acts 3:21

Romans 8:19-22

We can no more understand what it will be like in heaven than a caterpillar can understand what it will be like to be a butterfly. But like the caterpillar we were created to be something more glorious and spectacular than we can possibly imagine in our earthbound existence. So you can erase from your mind any unappealing images of heaven that linger there. You will not be sentenced to an eternity of aimless lounging and perpetual choir practice. Heaven will be an amplification of your fondest dreams, the ultimate fulfillment of your deepest longings. It seems that the golden city of Revelation will be nestled in the forests and waterfalls of Eden. Thomas Wolfe was wrong; you can go home again.

When you arrive in heaven, you can expect to feel perfectly at home. It won't be like eating Sunday dinner at the boss's house, or like living under continual surveillance of an all-seeing eye. It will seem that everything has been custom designed specifically to your individual tastes, as if someone read your mind, designed and built the mansion you'd always dreamed of, then gave it to you for your birthday.

1 Corinthians
15:35-54

In heaven we will not be ghosts. We will have new, spiritual bodies. Some make the mistake of thinking that spiritual bodies means incorporeal bodies. But that is not the case. Spiritual means under the control or direction of the Spirit. Nothing spiritual can be done without a physical apparatus. Loving your neighbor is "spiritual" but meaningless unless you see your neighbor's needs and meet them, whether it is taking him food and medicine while he is sick or inviting him to church, which means employing your body to act on his behalf. We must not fall into the trap of thinking the body unimportant. We sometimes do injustice to the body, blaming it for all our sins (Is it your body's fault that you lose your temper, snub an associate, or swell with pride?) and placing it at the bottom of the hierarchy when we speak of the three components — spirit, soul, and body — that make up our being. God designed the human creature to be an integrated unit, not a composite of three disconnectible parts. The body is essential to our humanity. It is the visible expression of our invisible self. The spirit without the body is impotent — incapable of action, communication, or making itself known. One of the worst hells we could imagine is being eternally bodiless and aware of nothing but our own existence — no light, no sense of presence, no sense of the existence of other beings, no way to know anything at all other than the dark, isolated, existence of a blind, unfeeling, unhearing, inactive, inexpressible self. Make no mistake; the body is important. It is to be redeemed. God has gone to incredible lengths to see that we will have eternal bodies because, more incredibly, the body is designed not only to display the invisible inner self; it is given the exalted honor of displaying the nature of the invisible God.

Romans 8:23

In our future existence we will have the same familiar bodies we have now, but with all their flaws and weaknesses corrected. Our bodies will be solid, flesh-and-bone organisms with all five senses intact and working, but they will be immune to pain, disease, age, and death. They will be like the bodies of the unfallen Adam and Eve, and like the body of Jesus after his Resurrection.

John 20:27,28
John 21:12,14
Philippians 3:20,21

Some religions teach that the ultimate achievement of human existence is to reach a state where we are completely free of all desire. On the surface, this seems to be a commendable goal, since our desires lead us into most of our troubles. But Christianity teaches that the purpose of all desire is to lead us to God. Therefore, the ultimate achievement for the

Christian is fulfillment, not repudiation of desire. We will not lay aside our desires when we enter heaven; that would be like leaving the hooks off our fishing lines. It is through the satisfaction of desire that we experience the ecstasy heaven offers.

Luke 19:17
1 Corinthians 6:1-3
2 Timothy 2:12
Revelation 3:21;
20:4
Daniel 12:3

Such dynamic new bodies recharged with properly aimed desires are not meant just to loll around heaven all day. Heaven will not be an elaborate retirement center; it will be a place of meaning and activity. What will we do there? The Bible is not specific, but it does drop a few tantalizing hints. It tells us that we will be in highly responsible positions. We will judge angels. We will be rulers — of what, the Bible does not say. We could flesh out the skeletons of these hints with our own guesses, but such an exercise would be futile. It is likely that God does not reveal more because our imaginations are not capable of handling the scope of the reality. Or maybe he just wants to surprise us. For now we must be content to know that whatever task God has in store will be the very thing we always wanted to do. It will eternally satisfy the deepest longings of our hearts.

What Is In the Future?

Hebrews 9:27
2 Corinthians 5:10
Revelation 20:11-15

Luke 23:43

1 Corinthians
15:20,51

1 Thessalonians
4:16-18
Revelation 22:12

Each of us must face death, and after death, God's judgment. Where will we be in the time between death and judgment? The Bible does not say. Some think that Jesus' answer to the thief on the cross means we will spend the time in an interim state — the place Jesus called Paradise. However, this option presents some problems because it seems to indicate that people are pretty much judged at death, rather than having to wait for judgment. And perhaps this is the case. Others think we will go into some sort of sleeplike state until the end of the world, at which we will all gather for the great judgment. Some have speculated that since God controls time and eternity, no matter when we die by earth's chronology, we will all seem to have arrived at judgment at the same time.

The Bible may be vague on some things, but it does clearly teach that Jesus is coming again, and that all God's people will be taken into heaven to live with him forever. However, Christians differ widely over just how and when these last events will occur. There are several "isms," each with its own timetable and sequence of events that seem to mark the end times and the Second Coming of Jesus. It is not the purpose of this book to attack or defend any of these positions. We will leave that task to others and try to stick to a simple explanation of what the Bible reveals without indulging in interpretation about sequences and specific times.

Matthew 24:27,36,42
1 Thessalonians 5:2
1 Thessalonians 4:16
Revelation 1:7

Jesus will appear suddenly at a moment when no one expects him. His arrival will be announced by the voice of an archangel and a trumpet blast that will be heard around the world. Everyone alive will see Jesus when he comes.

Rumors crop up now and then that Jesus is already here, living in some remote country and waiting for the right moment to reveal himself. But Christians need not worry about being fooled by rumors or impostors. The Bible tells us that he will come suddenly and spectacularly, and everyone will see him.

1 Thessalonians 4:16-18

The graves of the earth will open and give up the Christian dead in them. Then the Christians who are still alive when Jesus comes will rise up into the clouds with the risen dead to meet Jesus in the air. From there they will go to their new homes in heaven, where they will live forever.

These events are often called the end times, as if they signaled the end of the human story. But the story as God originally outlined it has not yet been written. Adam and Eve began the first chapter but spilled the ink over the remaining pages. Jesus has blotted the ink and cleaned the pages, and when he comes, he will present them to us to complete the story as it should have been written. Our story is not ending; it is about to begin.

Questions for Discussion: Chapter 13

1. Why aren't more people enthusiastic about heaven?

2. What kind of body can we expect to have in heaven?

3. Are our desires meant to be suppressed?

4. Why does the Bible say that God will remake the earth?

5. What do you think heaven will be like? Why?

6. Will we know when Jesus comes again?

About the Author

Tom Williams is an elder with the Garden Ridge Church of Christ and has been employed by Word Publishing in Dallas, Texas since 1988, currently the Executive Art Director. Tom had been the Art Director for Sweet Publishing from 1972 to 1976. As owner of his own art studio from 1976 to 1988, he designed over 1500 book covers for several Christian publishers including Zondervan, Moody, Eerdmans, Crossway and Baker. His cover designs have won national acclaim through the Christian Booksellers Association. He is a four-time winner of CBA's best book jacket award (twice as designer; twice as art director). His portrait of C.S. Lewis is displayed in the Wade Collection, the Lewis Library at Wheaton College, Illinois.

Tom is the author of three previous books: *See No Evil: Christian Attitudes Toward Sex in Art and Entertainment* published by Zondervan, *The Day Before the Downpour and Other Plays* published by Lillenas, *Divine Comedies: Plays for Christian Theater* by Meriwether, and one short play in a collection by Word Music. He has also written articles for *The Christian Appeal*, *Gospel Tidings*, and *The Christian Chronicle*.

Tom has been married to his wife, Faye, for 36 years and together they have three married daughters and eight grandchildren. He enjoys painting, writing, traveling, antiquing, listening to classical music and Broadway show scores, and reading.